PEARSON

ALWAYS LEARNING

Student Success and Career Development
SLS 1106

Compiled by Professor Lottie M. Tucker-McMillan

Custom Edition for Miami Dade College North Campus

Taken from:
College Orientation
by Karen Bendersky, PhD and Catherine M. Chastain-Elliott, PhD

The College Experience, Compact, First Edition
by Amy Baldwin and Brian Tietje

Pearson Learning Solutions, 501 Boylston Street, Suite 900, Boston, MA 02116
A Pearson Education Company
www.pearsoned.com

Printed in the United States of America

1 2 3 4 5 6 7 8 9 10 V092 16 15 14

000200010271908645

JHA

ISBN 10: 1-269-75476-9
ISBN 13: 978-1-269-75476-7

Course number: **SLS 1106**

Course Name: *First Year Experience Seminar*

Course Description: *This required Seminar is designed to provide new students (College Ready) with a forum for transitioning into college. Students will learn to develop the skills required for success in a college environment and beyond. (1cr.)*

Table of Contents

Chapters 1–5 taken from *College Orientation* by Karen Bendersky, PhD and Catherine M. Chastain-Elliott, PhD and Chapters 6–9 taken from *The College Experience, Compact*, First Edition by Amy Baldwin and Brian Tietje

Student Success and Career Development: A Custom Edition for Miami Dade College, North Campus SLS 1106, was compiled by Professor Lottie M. Tucker-McMillan, M.Ed.

Student Success and Career Development is A Custom Edition for SLS 1106, First Year Experience Seminar in Student *Life Skills*, (SLS), at Miami Dade College, North Campus in Miami, FL and was compiled by Professor ***Lottie M. Tucker-McMillan, M.Ed***. She is an Associate Professor of Education and Student Life Skills at the North Campus, Miami Dade College in Miami, FL. She is a "Master Teacher" and honored as "A Distinguished Educator" by Delta Sigma Theta Sorority, Inc. She is committed to teaching, student success and lifelong learning and has an extensive background in higher education administration, teaching, researching and severed in various roles at Miami Dade College, Miami, FL. She began her career as an Adjunct Professor in the School of Business at Wolfson Campus and taught business technology classes. She served as the first Director of Education at the Carrie P. Entrepreneurial Education Center, at North Campus from 1988 – 1990 and developed the curriculum for College Preparatory, AA/AS Degrees, Vocational Training and continued to teach technology courses for businessmen and lawyers from across the community who requested her Saturday morning technology classes. She has taught and developed the Educational Technology Courses, at North Campus in the School of Education, and integrated Live-Text Technology required for building student electronic portfolios for Florida's Teacher Certification. Professor McMillan has taught and developed Student Life Skills Seminars, Career and Business Seminars at North Campus. She developed the SLS 1401 Career and University Transfer Course and published it in 1992 in the North Campus first SLS Custom Textbook ***Keys to Excellence*** by Carol Cooper . Her research in 2007 includes 21st ***Century Strategies for Integrating Educational Technology into Student Life Skills Courses***, at North Campus. She has integrated Pearson's My Student Success Lab in several Student Life Skills Seminars and Courses. She participates in the development of the College-wide SLS curriculum and assists with SLS adjunct faculty training for My Student Success Lab at North Campus .

Professor McMillan continues to make outstanding contributions to *student success* at Miami Dade College, North Campus. She has a Master's Degree in Education, and Certificates in Education, Adult Educational Psychology, Entrepreneurial Management, Higher Education Administration and Educational Technology. She has a Bachelor's Degree in Business Teacher Education from Rust College and began her teaching career at Blayton Business College, in Atlanta, GA and taught Business Technology and Business Management Courses. Thereafter, she moved into middle management in higher education but she always taught a variety of subjects requested by students. She developed CDA training for Head Start Programs in northern Mississippi. She was Director of Education for the US Department of Labor Job Corps Center in Batesville, MS and also taught advanced mathematics. She joined the faculty at Florida Memorial University, Miami, FL in 1982 and served in dual roles as administrator and Professor of Education including College Registrar and developed the first computerized college-wide Registration and Academic Advisement Programs. She is a former Director, Associate Director, and Advisor of Student Financial Aid at Florida Memorial University and coordinated the college work study and scholarship programs on campus and supervised the FMC financial aid programs in the outreach centers in Hialeah, Liberty City and Little Haiti communities. As the Assistant to the Academic Dean at Florida Memorial College, she was responsible for the coordination of institutional research projects and worked closely with the, Southern Association of Colleges and Schools accreditation agency. Professor McMillan's is a former entrepreneur and co-owner of retail shops at the Bayside Market Place in Miami, FL and developed marketing strategies and managed inventory for retail sales. She is a member of the Carol City Steppers-Line Dancers and integrates these skills when developing strategies for teaching multiple intelligences in Student Life Skills Seminars and Courses. She has served as Secretary to the Board Directors of the Martin Luther King Economic Development Corporation, Inc., Miami, FL and educational consultants for various community organizations. She is a member of Delta *Sigma Sorority*, Inc. and past member of the *International Society for Technology in Education* and is an advocate for integrating educational technology in educational curriculums. She is involved in campus and community activities and is affectionately known as *DIVIA*. She is a *mentor* for her students who are successful in various career fields throughout the USA, including teachers in Broward and Dade Counties, aviators and officer in the USA Army, medical doctors, lawyers, Administrators in Higher Education and Corp America.

PREFACE
By Professor Lottie M. Tucker-McMillan, M.Ed.

The faculty in **Student Life Skills (SLS)** at Miami Dade College, North Campus, is committed to our 21st century College Ready Students, who have the knowledge, skills, and academic preparation needed to enroll and succeed in college courses in various career fields. College is much different from high school and students will need to develop good note-taking skills and time management skills, research information, and use campus resources. Students will be expected to choose a major that matches their skills, interests, personality and develop transferrable skills required in college and in various career fields.

Acknowledging that College Ready Students may need to focus on a few specific skills, the faculty in SLS at Miami Dade College, North Campus has *partnered* with Pearson and published **Student Success and Career Development: A Custom Edition**, for Miami Dade College, North Campus SLS 1106 for our First Year Experience Seminar. The textbook is integrated with **My Student Success Lab** technology, and includes over nineteen learning modules, various assessments tools, pre-test, post-test, interactive practices, video testimonies by students, journals, and essays that will help students to assess their knowledge and to focus on specific areas where they need more skills and develop critical thinking skills and much more. This textbook includes questions and answers that will help students to make a successful transition in the college. A former student in SLS at North Campus referred to her success by stating the following:

> *Every student entering college for the first time needs to take a College Orientation Seminar because just knowing the academics alone is not enough to help one adjust to the college environment. (Sarah Fox, April 25, 2014)*

Students should not be afraid of their new college environment because the distinguished faculty in SLS are experienced in various career fields and roles at the college and dedicated to student success. Students are expected to develop SMART goals that will help them to balance their time and become involved with campus activities, clubs, and organizations that will help them to develop leadership skills. College is also the time and place where students will establish their own values and become responsible adults.

Some important features in **Student Success and Career Development: A Custom Edition** include research by Dr. Karen Bendersky, Ph.D. and Catherine M. Chastain-Elliott, Ph.D., authors of **College Orientation**; and Amy Baldwin and Brain Tietje, authors of **The College Experience**. Our faculty has selected their research and aligned it with the three competencies for our SLS 1106, First Year Experience Seminar, and Miami Dade College **Learning Outcome #4**. Students will be expected to purchase the **Student Success and Career Development: A Custom Edition** at the North Campus bookstore.

Learning Outcome #4:   Information Literacy—Formulate strategies to locate, evaluate, and apply information.

The SLS 1106 Course Competencies:

> *Competency #1:   The student will demonstrate knowledge of college matriculation processes and procedures by:*

- Demonstrating knowledge of registration procedures, degree requirements, advisement services, financial aid, and the Standards of Academic Progress
- Identifying resources available at the college for successful academic progress, including identifying and explaining the importance of the 10 MDC Learning Outcomes
- Interpreting attendance and grading policies, and student rights and responsibilities
- Describing and applying the registration procedures including degree audit, adding and dropping courses, official withdrawal policies, and transcripts

Competency #2:   *The student will demonstrate utilization of effective study skills by:*

- Assessing his/her personal learning style and study skills
- Applying effective study skills
- Developing strategies for critical thinking, memory enhancement, and test-taking
- Identifying useful time management systems
- Applying knowledge of efficient note-taking skills, including active listening, organizing, and recording

Competency #3:   *The student will increase self-awareness and improve career decision-making by:*

- Identifying his/her personal characteristics including interests and abilities
- Evaluating and comparing various career options and their requirements
- Constructing a career plan that matches personal characteristics to career requirements
- Applying effective study skills
- Developing strategies for critical thinking, memory enhancement, and test-taking
- Identifying useful time management systems
- Applying knowledge of efficient note-taking skills, including active listening, organizing, and recording

DEDICATION

Our ***Student Success & Career Development Custom Textbook***, is dedicated to our "College Ready Students" who are enrolling in our new *SLS 1106*, First Year Experience Seminar at Miami Dade College, North Campus.

ACKNOWLEDGEMENTS AND GRATITUDE

The faculty wishes to thank the students for sharing their pictures and everyone at Pearson for supporting and working with us in developing our *Custom Student Success & Career Development Textbook* compiled for SLS 1106, Student Life Skills Seminar, First Year Experience, Miami Dade College, North Campus:

MDC Students

Rachel Buscemi

Christy Humeniuk

Amy Judd

Tara Tripp

Michelle Morgan

Jill Haber Atkins

The beautiful Lake on the Campus of MDC, North, Miami, FL

WELCOME!

By Dr. Nora Hernandez Hendrix, Ph.D. and Professor Lottie M. Tucker-McMillan, M. Ed.

Hello Students,

Welcome and thank you for choosing the North Campus of Miami Dade College – the first campus of Miami Dade College, established in 1960. We are pleased that you are enrolled in this Student Life Skills course because we know that it will contribute to your academic success and it will enrich your college experience. Our Student Life Skills (SLS) Professors have years of college teaching experience and have expertise in the fields of Education, Psychology and Counseling. We have also served in multiple roles at Miami Dade College including Academic and Student Dean, Campus President, Academic Advisor, Student Life Advisor, and Student Organization Advisor, and we have been recognized with numerous prestigious awards such as Master Teacher and Endowed Teaching Chair. We are delighted to offer our years of experience and our expertise to the students in SLS 1106, First Year Experience Seminar. This Custom Textbook was designed especially for you. It is our sincere hope that this textbook and this course will mark the beginning of many future successes as you pursue your academic and career goals.

The Faculty Committee for Student Life Skills (SLS)
Miami Dade College, North Campus

By Professor Lottie M. Tucker-McMillan, M. Ed.

Seated:

Professor Ginny Tennant-Peterson, Ph.D.

Professor Nora Hendrix, Ph.D.

Standing:

Professor Arlene Garcia, Ph.D.

Professor Lottie M. Tucker-McMillan, M.Ed.

Professor Valarie De Angelis, M. Ed.

Not pictured:

Professor Jamie Anzalotta, M.S.W.

Professor Sheryl Hartman, Ph.D.

BREAKTHROUGH
To improving results

MyStudentSuccessLab™

Help students start strong and finish stronger.

Engaging Experiences   Improving Results   Partner

MyStudentSuccessLab helps students to "Start strong, Finish stronger" by acquiring the skills they need to succeed for ongoing personal and professional development through peer-led video interviews, interactive practice exercises, and activities. Developed exclusively for Pearson, the *Conley Readiness Index* by Dr. David Conley is embedded within MyStudentSuccessLab as a research-based, self-diagnostic that measures college and career readiness. Together, the *Conley Readiness Index* and MyStudentSuccessLab create a powerful learning tool with behavioral and knowledge-based assessment focused on the whole student. There are also title-specific courses available that include an eText, align the Learning Path to the book, and provide chapter assessments.

Students have access to:

- **Full Course Pre- and Post-Diagnostic Assessments** linked to key learning outcomes

- **Pre- and Post-Tests** dedicated to individual topics in the Learning Path

- **Overviews** that summarize the skills found in the practice exercises and activities for the topic

- **Videos on key issues** that are "by students, for students," conveniently organized by topic

- **Practice exercises** that build student confidence before completing the graded activities

- **Graded activities** to build critical-thinking and problem-solving skills

www.mystudentsuccesslab.com

Get Started with Pearson's MyStudentSuccessLab

First, make sure you have these 3 things...

Email: You'll get some important emails from your instructor at this address.

Course ID: A Course ID looks something like this: professor12345

Access code or credit card: The required access code comes either with your book or by itself at your bookstore. Alternatively, you can buy instant access with a credit card or PayPal account during registration.

Next, get registered!

1. Go to **www.pearsonmylabandmastering.com**.

2. Under the large **Register** section on the right side of the page, and click the **Student** button.

3. Read the onscreen instructions and click **OK! Register now.**

4. Next, enter the **Course ID** for your course (listed above).

5. After this, either **Create** a new Pearson username and password, or, if you've already registered for another Pearson product (i.e. MyMathLab), **Sign In** with that username and password.

6. On the next page, click the **Access Code** button if you purchased a package with an access code sfrom the bookstore, OR purchase instant access now by clicking on the purchase options under the **Use a Credit Card or PayPal** section.

7. You are now registered! Now, it's time to sign. Go to **www.pearsonmylabandmastering.com** and click the **Sign In** button in the top right. Enter your username and password.

Need help?

Visit www.mystudentsuccesslab.com/get-registered for:

- Helpful videos
- Frequently Asked Questions
- System Requirements
- Other helpful "getting started" info!

Or visit our 24/7 Technical Support site at http://247pearsoned.custhelp.com.

How Are Expectations Different in College?

1

Like you, most freshmen entering college have a general sense of what college is all about. They know they will take classes, study, spend time in **extracurricular activities** (college-sponsored nonacademic activities like sports and clubs), earn grades, and make friends. But is college really different from high school? It is, but not in terms of the types of activities. The real differences lie within each activity. The transition from high school to college is difficult for most students—even those who know there will be differences. To prepare yourself to cope with these differences, take note of the expectations outlined in this section.

As a high school senior, you probably had certain privileges and rights designed to provide you with more freedom than your younger peers. Maybe you were allowed to arrive later in the morning, go off campus for lunch, or skip certain events. Arriving at college, you will find that this freedom increases exponentially. In fact, there are very few restrictions placed on how you spend your day. This is because your professors and college administrators view you as an adult. As exhilarating as this may sound, this abrupt change in how you are viewed can be overwhelming. To be successful in college, it is important to understand your new freedom and to view it as an important step in your development. Appreciate it for what it is, and make the most of it; otherwise, it may make the most of you! Start each day with a plan. Make a list of specific tasks that you need to accomplish, and organize your commitments (including both class time and extra study time) in a planner or in your phone's calendar system.

Professor Nora Hernandez Heidrix, PhD

Image courtesy of Miami Dade College - North Campus

From Session 1 of *College Orientation*, First Edition. Karen Bendersky, Catherine M. Chastain-Elliott.

Do I Really Get a Three-Day Weekend?
SMART USE OF CLASS SCHEDULES AND MORE FREE TIME

The university course schedule is very different from high school. In high school, you probably started early in the morning and then took six hours of classes every day. College courses are usually assigned a Monday, Wednesday, and Friday (MWF) or Tuesday and Thursday (TR) schedule. Your Introduction to Psychology course might meet only on MWF or it might meet only on TR. This means you will have some classes on some days of the week and not others. It also could mean you have entire days without classes if all of your classes are only on Mondays, Wednesdays, and Fridays, or Tuesdays and Thursdays. It just depends on what is offered during the **term** (i.e., semester or quarter). The classes and your schedule will vary from term to term. Sometimes, you will have a day when classes begin at 8:00 A.M. Sometimes, your first class of the day might start at 4:30 P.M.

Due to this scheduling, you might find yourself with more time outside of class than you had in high school. Students generally love having so much free time, and they often find their sleep schedule changing due to late morning classes and opportunities for naps. It is nice to be in class less, but having more time to schedule on your own can also hurt you. You might allow yourself to skip a class because it is the only one scheduled on a certain day and you want that entire day to yourself. You might convince yourself to procrastinate on a project because it seems you have so much time in the future to get it done. Use your unscheduled time wisely. In general, it is important to realize that time between classes is not truly free. Course homework for college classes, though assigned less often than in high school, is more in depth and can have a much longer completion timeframe. For example, it is common for an assignment to be handed out on the first day of class and due on the last. Some students find that they operate better, and are more academically successful, if they have less free time. Why? Because when your schedule is full, you realize you have to get things done earlier and do not have the luxury of procrastinating. If you are a procrastinator, you might consider filling some of your nonclass time with other commitments so that you stay on task (and do not sleep in). Working on long-term projects, such as research papers, that are due at the end of the term should be your main between-classes commitment.

Luckily, there are scheduling tools that can keep you from feeling overwhelmed or from procrastinating. These tools can seem so simplistic that you might dismiss them, but we guarantee that they really work and will save you time later. As a college student, you are actually juggling multiple time roles including class time, self time, social time, and study time. Later, when you transition into your postgraduation time roles (e.g., job time, self time, social time, and family time), you will find yourself more and more dependent on these tools. Getting in the habit of using them will serve you well now and later.

Table 1 Helpful Scheduling and Organizing Tools

Tool	Type	What and Why	Best for Students Who...
Scheduling	Daily Planner	• traditional paper planners • keeps you from missing assignments, tests, classes, and events • helps you plan and get your work done early	• like the feel of flipping pages and writing things in • are self-motivated enough to check their planner daily and always carry it with them
	Phone Calendar	• calendar function on your phone (smart or other type; recommend using alarm or pop-up reminder functions) • keeps you from missing assignments, tests, class, and events • helps you plan and get your work done early	• never leave home without their phone • are willing to program in all events • are not good with planners
Organizing	To-Do Lists	• a list of things that need to get done (electronic or on paper) • they free up your memory for other tasks • promotes feelings of accomplishment every time you cross off a task	• need a quick way to reduce stress • will not make lists that are too broad (e.g., "Write English 101 paper") • will list mini-steps to a larger final product (e.g., "Develop thesis statement for English 101 paper")
	Course Folders/ Binders	• folders or binders holding information organized by course (History 101) or by content (My Syllabi) • organizing by course allows monitoring of course progress	• are disorganized • do not usually monitor their course progress

Did I Actually Miss Six Classes?
KEEPING TRACK OF YOURSELF AND YOUR WORK

In high school, your teachers probably kept track of your work, your absences, and you. If you missed a class, they noticed. If you did not turn in an assignment, they reminded you to turn it in. They knew your name. If your grades started to slip, they would talk with you about it or have a parent–teacher conference. College is completely different.

In classes requiring attendance, if you miss a class, it will be recorded but not necessarily noticed. Some classes do not even require attendance. It will be up to you to come to class. Professors will not ask you why you were not there, nor will they want to know (in many cases). This has nothing to do with not caring about you; it has everything to do with fostering independence. You are now going to be treated as an adult who has the personal responsibility of making it to class. This is not the professor's responsibility.

What about failing to turn in an assignment? Expect the same response. That is, the professor will record a 0 and that is it. No reminders. At the end of the term, the professor will simply record a grade of F. Do not expect to be reminded of your due dates or asked to track down your missing assignments. Most assignment due dates are listed on a **syllabus** (an instructor's course summary document listing contact information and the course schedule and requirements) or online. There is little handholding in college, and tears do not work. One math professor we know actually recommended to his fellow faculty that they should "let them cry." Although this remark seems insensitive, the point is that you are on your own, and your professors want you to learn how to be successful on your own. You certainly would not want to use tears as a strategy with your boss at work. Use college to work out alternative ways to deal with deadlines and pressures.

Can you make up missed assignments at the end of the term? Generally, no; it is too late. It is considered inconsiderate to ask a professor to provide special accommodations just for you. The end of the term is an extremely busy time for professors, and many have little tolerance for students who did not put in the effort or plan in advance.

Can I Get Up and Leave?
PRACTICING PROFESSIONAL CLASSROOM BEHAVIOR

The classroom environment in college is different, too. While professors expect respect from their students and a certain level of decorum, there is also a level of flexibility that likely did not exist in high school. This balance may seem odd at first, and it may take some getting used to. The most important point to remember is that your behavior should not disrupt your peers or your professor.

As a college student, plan to get to class on time (if not early), refrain from talking to others during lectures, and familiarize yourself with and follow the rules outlined in the class syllabus. If you are late, expect that you have lost the rights to your seat. This means entering the classroom from the back, if possible, and finding the seat closest to the door. Never walk in front of or behind the professor while he or she is lecturing. Can you imagine a late stagehand walking behind Stephen Colbert during the taping of his show? To professors, this type of student disruption is just as disrespectful. We have known several professors who will even lock the classroom door in order to handle tardiness. If a student is late, he or she is not allowed to enter the classroom. While we definitely think this solution is extreme, most instructors (and students) understand the professor's frustration with late entrances.

During class, questions that are appropriate to the material are always welcome (e.g., "Did Frank Lloyd Wright build *prairie-style* homes in other areas of the country besides the Midwest?"). Asking random questions is inappropriate, even if they seem to relate to the topic (e.g., asking in a psychology course, "My mother always…is this why I am anxious now as an adult?"). Why might such a question be inappropriate? It is a very personal question that relates to one person only. It does not further discussion and would become a dialog between the individual student and the professor, rather than between the professor and the class as a whole. Questions like this would be better saved for after class (or for a therapist, in this case). Another example of a random question would be stopping a lecture or discussion to ask the meaning of a term. If the word is a new term related to the topic, it will be defined by the professor or will be found in your course materials or text. If it is simply a word that you have never heard, jot it down in the margin and look it up after class.

In college classrooms, you do not have to raise your hand to leave the classroom. If you need to go to the bathroom, by all means please go. If you have a coughing fit, please go get a drink of water. It is best to take care of personal business before getting to class. Use the restroom, bring water or cough drops if you have a cough, make any phone calls or send any text messages before you enter the classroom. Getting up to leave is a distraction not only for the professor, who faces the class and sees everything that goes on, but also for other students who are trying to concentrate.

As a last point, you may be surprised to find that most professors will allow food in the classroom. This is not usually the case in high school. There is often limited time between classes, and some schedules may not allow time for lunch. You may drink coffee, eat your donut, or even consume an entire meal while taking notes. Show respect by asking the professor if it is okay first. Some may mind due to the nature of what is going on in the class (food spilled on a computer in a digital arts class, for instance, will ruin the equipment). Of course, be mindful of the type of food you bring. For instance, you would not want to bring anything noisy, like potato chips or crunchy carrots. You will only distract your classmates. The overall message is that you should not interrupt the flow of what is happening in the classroom.

Is This Class Really This Easy?
THE EXPECTATION THAT YOU CHALLENGE YOURSELF

The big secret is that college is not necessarily difficult (after all, you most likely got into a college appropriate to your level), but the expectations are certainly much higher. You will have to work harder even in areas that you may have special talent. Professors assume you understand how to act in class, know how to study, and know how to write. They assume you have basic knowledge in several key academic areas and that you are self-motivated to study and do the work assigned; otherwise you would not be here. They also assume you can handle critique and criticism. Most professors believe you want to learn and that you know that learning requires a fair amount of critiquing of your work. Gratification comes from working hard to master the material and gaining new confidence in your abilities.

Many students complain that freshmen courses are not challenging, that high school seemed harder. Conversely, many professors complain that freshmen are unprepared. There is some obvious disconnect here. We think this disconnect is due to differing expectations. Students expect more to happen in class and to be given more to do outside class. Professors expect more to happen outside of class, but without direction. Take the case of a first-year literature course. One English professor we know would love to have lively discussions about the books he assigns for his class. His students could debate the themes in the books, analyze characters, create and defend theses, etc. The problem is that few read the books before class. They expect the professor to teach them the book, while the professor expects the students to come to class with the book read and already studied. This professor has found that in order to talk about the book, he has to give quizzes to ensure his students have the book read by class time. You can see the lack of rigor in this example is due to a complicated interaction between the students' behavior and the professor's expectations. **Challenge** (working at and above one's intellectual comfort level) begins with the student. If you and your peers do not prepare for class, your professor may respond by altering what goes on in class in ways that might make class time less stimulating for you.

Was That a Trick Question?
LEARNING THE MEANING OF COLLEGE STUDYING

Why study? Some students do not feel the need to study because they did not always need to study to do well in high school. Due to grade inflation and a variety of new ways to calculate grade point averages (GPA), some students even graduate from high school—with minimal studying—with a GPA above 4.0. At the college level, it is extremely rare to achieve a 4.0. A 4.0 in college is considered perfect. Graduating from high school with little studying, and with such elevated GPAs, has set up unfortunate expectations for some students.

All students, including the very best, need to know how to study in college. We asked a sample of high school teachers the one greatest misconception high school students have about college. Their overwhelming answer was this: High school students think they know how to study. The implication is that students are doing something that they consider to be studying, but that teachers and professors do not think is studying. Remember, just because your study method in high school got you the grade, it does not mean that method will work in college. In fact, the students who do best in college are the ones with a solid understanding of what constitutes true studying, and not the ones who just **matriculate** (enter college) with top grades. We've seen students who arrive at college with a 4.0 fail miserably, while students who worked extremely hard for a 3.2, finish their first term with A's and B's. So, what activities are considered studying? Here is our list of activities often misunderstood to be studying:

1. You consider reading the textbook (or other reading assignment) to be studying.
2. You consider reading the textbook (or other reading assignment) while highlighting important information to be studying.
3. You consider reading over your notes before the exam to be studying.
4. You consider typing up your handwritten notes to be studying.
5. You consider simply completing all of the assignments to be studying.

The most notable advice from your upper-level peers is to study. Your courses will be more interesting and challenging if you do study the material. To truly retain and learn information for the long term, you need to engage in additional types of activities. It is important to study the right way, because explaining to your professor that you "worked so hard to get a good grade on the exam"—will not change a low grade.

What Is True Studying?

In college, you will have homework and reading assignments. Doing homework is not the same as studying. Reading is not the same as studying. These two activities are necessary, but they are not the same thing as studying. They are what you do *before* you study. Doing homework and reading are just the first step. Professors will not teach you how to study; they expect you to come to college knowing what activities will help you learn.

True studying involves the long-term conscious effort to learn, understand, and memorize material. Long-term is not measured in hours. It is measured in weeks (sometimes years). It is something that needs to be done daily. It requires a great amount of effort and focus. Quality studying involves doing extra problems and testing yourself. Use the end-of-chapter questions given to you in your textbooks. If you want to learn the material in a math class, you have to take notes in class, read the material in the book, and do the practice problems, but these are only the precursors to studying. The next step is making sure that you have retained the information by testing yourself—honestly. Without looking at your notes and the book, can you explain the math problems to someone else? If not, you really do not know or understand the material.

This is one technique for determining whether you have to study more. This means going back through your notes, reviewing the textbook, doing more problems, and retesting yourself. Recognizing what you do not know or understand is an important part of the studying process. When you study, make the material specific to what you know already or to you personally. This is possible with any subject. For example, in a statistics course covering probability, you might think: "At some point in my future, I might want to understand the probability of dying if I take a certain amount of a particular drug; how do I understand this?" You can even apply this strategy to world literature. Can you explain the reading or story to someone else? Do you know and remember the main characters? What was the author's intent in writing the story? Was the author's theme driven by personal experience or historical context? It really does not matter whether your answers to these questions are accurate at the outset. What matters is that you are considering these questions as you reread the stories. Just the act of spending more time thoughtfully reflecting on the material leads to (and counts as) studying.

There are different ways to study. For short-term studying, you might **cram** (do all of your studying in a single time period, like the night before the exam). We do not advocate cramming. Admittedly, it might get you a passing grade, but you will not remember the information long term. This can be a problem, especially in fields (like chemistry or math) that build on earlier courses. To really retain information, you will have to engage in distributed repetition studying rather than mass repetition. **Distributed repetition** involves studying a little every day over the course of the term. Once this becomes habit, it is easy to do. Set a specific schedule for studying. For example, depending on your schedule, you might set aside every MWF from 1–3 P.M. and every TR from 8–10 P.M. as your study/course-work time; others might prefer devoting their entire weekends to study. **Mass repetition studying** is just a fancy term for cramming. It involves memorizing (through rehearsal) all the study material at one time (for example, the night before the exam). We of course recommend the distributed repetition method. Now, how exactly do you study this way?

Following is a basic study goals list to get you started. Do everything listed, particularly if you are struggling in a course. Do not pick and choose from the list. If you need additional help with studying, go to your college's academic tutoring center. These centers offer *free* tutoring.

Effective studying consists of the following activities:

1. **Hard work.** You may have heard "learning should be fun" during your K–12 years, but this philosophy is best suited for children (although children, too, should learn the value of hard work). Hard work comes from self-discipline. Beginning now, train yourself to quietly focus on your study tasks for blocks of time. The "fun" part comes when you have done your absolute best to master the material, and you know you have given it your all. Even if your hard work does not pay off in an A+ grade—something that is entirely possible in college—you will have achieved a new level of confidence in your abilities, especially if the

subject matter is challenging for you. The college experience is *purposefully designed* to do this for you, so use this opportunity. Your confidence will continue to grow as you tackle additional study tasks, and you will graduate a self-assured, well-rounded individual who feels comfortable tackling unfamiliar tasks (qualities that are extremely attractive to future employers).

2. **Reading your notes.** No matter what the subject, take thorough and copious notes, even if the professor posts his or her PowerPoint lectures or lecture outlines online. Pay special attention to the organization of lectures so you understand what material falls under what major headings/areas.

3. **Completing any gaps in your notes.** For example, fill in information if you missed a class or just missed something during lecture. Ask a friend or classmate for notes—preferably a very well-organized and fastidious student. Avoid asking your professor if you missed anything important on a certain date. Take responsibility for getting yourself updated and informed.

4. **Memorizing.** Memorize important terms/information, using whatever method works for you: note cards, retyping your notes, or another method.

5. **Creating unique examples.** Create new examples of the terms and information (the more personally relevant the better); do not simply parrot the text or the professor's examples. For instance, if you just learned that *negative reinforcement* causes an increase in behavior due to the removal of an aversive (or bad) stimulus, come up with an example from your own experience: "I started taking a different bus to campus so I wouldn't run into my ex anymore."

6. **Formulating questions.** Ask yourself questions about key terms and information (what is this information, why is it important, who is it relevant to, when is it used?).

7. **Seeking clarification.** Identify information that is unclear or confusing and seek explanation if needed from the professor, a peer, or the tutoring center.

8. **Testing yourself.** Use the questions often found at the end of a text's chapter or, even better, create your own mini-test that follows the same format as the course exams.

9. **Teaching the material.** Once you feel confident that you have a firm grasp on the material, try teaching it to a peer. Alternately, offer to tutor a friend, or just see if you can teach it to an imaginary audience (do this without looking at your notes or the book). This is the ultimate test of your knowledge. If you can teach the material and handle questions others have about what you are teaching, you have mastered it.

10. **Avoiding too much group studying.** Students in a group may be ahead of or behind you and may waste your time. Plus, study groups tend to socialize during sessions, which may also waste time. If you want to participate in a study group, follow steps 1–9 before joining the group. Once you meet, you will know what you need help with from the others and can exchange your self-tests.

Professor Nora Hernandez Heidrix, Ph.D.

Image courtesy of Miami Dade College - North Campus

Do not hesitate to ask for help. Professors would rather see you take the initiative to improve yourself than to founder on your own because of fear of being seen as weak or less smart. Alternatively, if you are particularly adept in a subject, consider working as a tutor on campus.

What Is the Secret to Reading Textbooks?

While you are reading an assigned text, do you periodically check to see how many more pages you have left? We thought so! You may have even done so with this text. But do you check the pages on a thriller novel you cannot put down? Probably not. Which book's information do you retain better? Usually the thriller novel. One of the reasons you remember the thriller better is that it follows a familiar schema. That is, you know what to expect as you are reading: introduction of main characters (with whom you might identify), twisted plot, climax, denouement, etc. It all fits neatly in your concept of a story. If asked to recount the story later, all you have to do is remember that it was a thriller and you have the cues you need to remember the rest. To read assigned texts more effectively, you should have a better sense of what to expect. You need to develop a **textbook schema** (your knowledge or concept of the kinds of information a textbook contains) because understanding how textbook authors write will act as a cue that will help you better remember the material.

Pay attention to the organization of the information in the text because it is an important cue you can use as you read. Your professor will usually present an organizational outline in his or her syllabus, so before you even look at the text, look over the syllabus. Note how the professor has divided the course (e.g., is the information organized topically or chronologically?). See what major areas are to be covered on each exam. Now, compare these major areas to the text. For example, you might notice that your course in developmental psychology is topically organized into three main themes: infant development, cognitive development, and social development. If the exam covers the cognitive development section, look in the text and see what topics are covered under that particular area. This is where your textbook schema begins for this class. You now know that your developmental text is topically organized. Next you should look at the subheadings within each of the major areas. See how the author breaks down the information. All authors follow a pattern when they write, and you should notice what it is. In the cognitive development subsections, the author might use the following organization: background/history of person/ theory, discussion of the person/theory, strengths of theory, criticisms of theory, and applications of theory. Under each of these sections are even more subheadings that will follow a specific pattern. If you know the author's text organization, you have your schema. When you need to remember information from the text, and as you study the text, remember this schema.

Just as authors use a particular organization, they too have a specific slant (or standpoint) on a subject. Sometimes, this slant will be obvious; sometimes, it will be more subtle. Professors will often choose a text that follows a view that matches their own. As you peruse the textbook, see if you can deduce the author's bias. Bias exists in all kinds of textbooks. In math, for instance, an author may be predisposed to students learning the theory behind different concepts (and so organize material in a theory/proof way) rather than learning the application of material (and focus on computation). You might think there is only one way to learn math concepts, but that is not necessarily so. If you can figure out the author's (and professor's) preference, you can start to ask more intelligent and challenging questions in class and have a better schema for when you study and recall information. If you are checking the page numbers of what you are reading, you are not really engaged in the material. Stop and take a break. Return to your reading when you have the time to get into the material and can really focus.

Some professors, especially in upper-level courses, might not use a textbook. Instead, they assign **journal articles** (original writings or research published in academic periodicals) and other primary reading materials. You can apply the preceding method to understanding journal articles. If you recall, the college curriculum is organized from broad coverage of information (World Civilization) to more specialized information (Intellectual History of Europe since 1550) as you progress into your major. This shift in coverage is often reflected in the assigned readings. Textbooks are assigned in lower-level courses because they offer good, basic, broad coverage of a given topic. They serve as an introduction to an entire field of study and are designated **secondary sources** because the information they contain is compiled from other **primary sources** (the original sources of information). Once you progress into specific topics within the field, textbooks will be replaced with specialized books or journal articles. Some of these books and journal articles might be primary sources. As you progress, you will learn the value of each source and the appropriateness of the source for a particular task. Colleges refer to this skill as **information literacy** (understanding how to find and use information). The textbook may be a great starting place for information on a topic that is new to you ("what is mitosis"), but it is not the best source if you need to understand the information at a deeper level ("how is mitosis affected by prenatal maternal ingestion of prednisolone") or if you are developing a hypothesis or thesis ("the interphase stage of mitosis is the most susceptible stage to prednisolone"). As you advance in your studies, you will become more information literate and appreciate the value of secondary and primary sources.

How Are Memorization and Application Different?

Memorization of material is the foundation of knowledge in every field. Forget what you have heard about **rote memorization** being useless; this is a required skill and will serve you well in college and in your career. Rote memorization involves rehearsing terms and their definitions to the extent that one can easily recite the definition when given the term, or identify the term when presented the definition. The average, or C, student, may stop here. If you aspire to achieve more, then take the next step in your studying and learn to apply the information.

Methods of memorization range from note cards with terms and definitions written on either side to covering notes with your hand and checking to see if you remember what is written underneath. You may use crazy-sounding stories or sentences to help. For instance, to memorize the date 1814 for a double portrait in an early American art history class, a student once told herself to remember that the first person in the painting was 18 years old, and the second was 14 which combine to signal the year 1814. While it was not true, the student was able to remember the date for years every time she saw the portrait because she remembered her story. Similarly, a landscape showing a forest from 1848 will "tell" you its date if you ask yourself to remember the—again, obviously untrue—story that it took *18* people to plant *48* of those trees.

Although memorization is the foundation of knowledge, it is only the first step toward mastery of the subject matter. The real test of your knowledge comes with application. Indeed, one important difference between high school and college exams is the expectation of professors that students apply their newly acquired knowledge, not simply recognize it.

Understanding the application of information takes more time and focus than rote memorization. We think you will find that it is much more interesting than working to remember a list of words and definitions. To explore the application of terms, ask yourself what their relevance is to the topic of study. Pay attention to what other terms and topics are related to it. Try to identify examples of these terms in your everyday life. Practice coming up with examples related to the terms. Imagine that you are given a short-answer question in which you must explain a term. You will receive an average grade for simply defining the term. For a more complete explanation, also include in your answer the relevance of the term to the topic as well as a clear example of the term.

This is an A-level college student answer that will distinguish you from those who are still performing at a high school level.

Do not fool yourself into thinking that only short answer or essay questions test your application abilities. Multiple-choice questions often do this, too, and these types of exams can be quite challenging. Such questions may begin with a scenario where you will be asked to identify the appropriate related term or information. When you study, assume that you will have to apply the information. Also, do not assume that the professor will show you how to apply the information. He or she will assume you are doing this when you study. He or she will teach the basic information you need to understand the material, but will not always teach you how to apply this material. That will be left for you to work out. This is, in truth, good training for real-world application where you will need to rely on your own creative ability to apply the basic work knowledge you have to novel work situations.

How Much Studying Am I Expected to Do?

We know a math professor who has broken down study time for his students. As a general rule, students in his class should be studying at least two to four hours every day—just for his class. The rule he uses is two to four hours of studying outside of class to every hour in class. If a class is fairly easy for you, use the lower amount. For some, math courses might be more challenging than others and so might require a longer time commitment, particularly if one is struggling. To be fair, with a 15–16 credit-hour load, four hours a day for one course does not leave a lot of time for web surfing, video game playing, or sitting on the beach. But take this general advice to heart, because good grades require you devote a good portion of each day to studying.

I Worked All Night on That Project! Why Didn't I Get an A?
GRADING IN COLLEGE

Grading in college is very different from high school. For one thing, professors are under little or no pressure to have to pass a certain number of students. If few students get A's, the assumption is that the students that term did not work very hard. Often, high school instructors must "teach to the test." They do this because they are evaluated by students' performance on the test. Poor student performance might translate to the teacher's lack of a raise—or lack of a job. Professors, for the most part, do not have this same type of pressure. They have the freedom to really challenge their students (i.e., require hard work) and to assign true grades. What are true grades? They are grades that are earned and are not based on effort.

One major adjustment you will have to make in college relates to earning a grade. This does not imply that you did not earn your grades in high school. You had to work hard in order to get as far as you have; however, you might have been given some slack that will not occur in college. Some examples of slack include a parent negotiating a better grade, being given the opportunity to receive extra credit, being allowed to retake a test or to turn in a missed assignment late, having a test review session or a review sheet, and being graded for effort.

Can Parents Negotiate or Affect a Grade?

Consider yourself lucky if your parent did not negotiate a grade for you in high school. We have actually heard stories of parents showing up in high school classrooms demanding to see copies of tests or to watch lectures. Please know that in college, parents simply do not have the same influence. Professors do not have to talk with parents; in fact, in most cases, professors cannot legally share information about a student's progress without the student's consent due to the Family Educational Rights and Privacy Act, **FERPA** (the government act restricting nonauthorized access to student academic records). Parents might call the department **chairperson** or **department head** (the person who heads an entire academic department), the **dean** (the person who oversees an entire academic school within the university), or the president, but none of those calls is going to get a grade changed. If anything, it might inadvertently backfire for the student. What kind of reputation is this student going to have among the other faculty members? Is this student able to solve problems on his or her own? We know many professors who will not even return a call from a parent. In these professors' minds, there is little to discuss, since any type of discussion could lead to a violation of your privacy. Plus, since a parent is not a participant in the class, how can he or she effectively speak for the student? A call from a parent will probably not get you what you want, and it may do more harm than good.

One difficult transition to college and adulthood is learning to take on the role of adult. This means taking full responsibility for yourself and your actions; a parent directly stepping in on your behalf can lead to a negative reputation. Similarly, and perhaps even more likely, is that a parent's well-intentioned behavior actually negatively influences the student's grade. Students often find it difficult to ignore phone calls and texts from their parents. Parents mean well; they want to check up on you or perhaps respond to your attempts to contact them. The issue is that current technology allows parents to get in contact with you *at will*. This means they can contact you while you are in class, while you are in a meeting with a professor, while you are working, or even while you are in an interview. Because texting a reply back or answering the phone is so automatic, you might find yourself doing so before you even realize what you have done. Most professors and offices have a policy regarding texting and phone use. Some professors may even drop you from a class with an F or W (withdrew) for violating this policy. Furthermore, texting in class only interferes with your ability to take notes and learn the course material, leading to a lower grade. The solution is often not easy for students. You might even have to turn off your phone. A good place to start is to give your parents a schedule of appropriate contact times.

One student we know spent an entire class period texting with his mom. He missed all of the relevant information, did not participate in discussions, and afterward found himself begging not to be dropped from the course for his violation. His dad was in the hospital, and his mother was sending him text updates. The problem was that his behavior interfered with the class (other students noticed, the professor had to verify his actions) and with his ability to get anything out of the class session. He, in fact, did have a valid excuse, but he did not handle it maturely. He should have contacted the professor before class. Had he done so, he would have been excused. This student really had two valid options:

1. he could fully assess the situation (is this situation worth loosing class information), opt to take an absence, and notify the professor, or

2. he could decide that it was not an emergency (he did not really need constant updates) and turn off his phone or tell his mother to call him in an hour after class was over.

Both options offer valid mature ways of handling the situation and are certainly preferable to a reduced grade. The bottom line is that in college, you will now have to make independent decisions that might affect your grade, and sometimes these decisions will force you to exert control over your parent.

Can I Get Extra Credit?

If your professor offers extra credit, consider it a gift. Not everyone offers extra credit. Some professors do not even believe in it. After all, the assignments and tests should be accurate assessments of your work. What, then, is the point of extra credit? Students should not ask a professor for extra credit at the end of the term (after grades are determined or after the final exam). At this point, the course is over. You had all term to accumulate points; a last-minute interest in improving your grade may be seen as insincere on your part.

Are Review Sessions Always Offered?

In high school, teachers might tell you what is on the exam. In such cases, a review session might make sense if that session includes a summary of key points that should be studied. In college, however, it is expected that you will figure out what is important and what the key topics are. Many professors do not understand the purpose of review sessions. After all, they already spent several weeks covering quite a bit of information. *Of course* all of the material is relevant and *of course* it will all be on the exam. What is there to cover in a review? In essence, requesting a review session asks professors to cover information already covered over a series of weeks. They have already taught the material, and they cannot possibly go over all of it again. Many students attend review sessions in hopes of learning what is "on the exam," but this expectation is erroneous. Remember that the purpose of the exam is to assess how much you know from the course. For obvious reasons, the professor cannot ask you to write down everything you know from the course. Instead, on the exam, your course knowledge is being *sampled*. The professor chooses one question from one specific knowledge area to "sample" whether you know information from that area. The more you know, the better the chance of having your specific knowledge sampled. If you know only a sampling of information, you do not really know an A-level amount of material.

Professor Nora Hernandez Heidrix, Ph.D.

Image courtesy of Miami Dade College - North Campus

Your professors offer study guides and study sessions? Well then, make use of them. Some professors will take questions directly from the study guide or study session and put them on their exams. When arriving for a review session, do not expect the professor to tell you what is on the exam or to give a mini-lecture. Most professors handle review sessions as a time for specific questions and answers. An appropriate review session question would be, "In the equation for the sample standard deviation, does one divide by n or $n - 1$?" The understanding here is that you have already started studying before the review session and are looking for clarification on items in your notes or in the text that seem fuzzy. An inappropriate question in a statistics course review would be, "I don't understand chapters two and three. Can you go over them?" Not understanding a whole section means you are in big trouble. Did you miss class that day? The professor undoubtedly covered that material and will not be able to justify spending a large chunk of the review time catching you up. It is your job to seek help during **office hours** (available times a professor sets aside specifically for meeting with students) if you missed class or were struggling with the material. Additionally, what does it mean to not understand an entire section? Be concrete in your questions. Review sessions are meant for clarification, not for tutoring.

Isn't There a Grade for Effort?

"But I worked really hard—harder than I ever have!" Saying so to an instructor will not lead to a grade change. In college, you get what you earn. You might be a really great person, but if you fail a test, you fail a test. Professors do not enjoy assigning a poor grade to a student whom they are fond of, but what are the other options? Professors work very hard to maintain fairness within a class. To grade based on effort would be unfair to the other students and will not help you in the long run. Simply put, should the person who studied the least, but performed very well on the exam, receive a lower grade? If a professor reinforces you for effort, what is the incentive to really learn how to study effectively? Remember, professors have your best interests at heart. In the workplace, your raise will not be determined by effort, only by results. Say that you work for a real estate firm. You did not make many sales one quarter, but you sure worked extraordinarily hard. Your coworker made record sales. Guess who will get the bonus?

Can I Challenge a Grade?

"What can I do if I have reason to challenge a grade I received on an assignment?" It is best to approach your professor pleasantly and with respect. Your professor is the only person who can change grades; neither the department chairperson nor even the dean has this power. Be prepared to present only the facts, and be open to the professor's explanation, because he or she gave you the grade for a reason and feels that it is legitimate.

Here is an example: A student states, "You said that this essay could cover a topic of our choice, and then you took off points for writing about an inappropriate topic." The professor responds, "I instructed you to write about a topic of your choice as long as it was covered in chapter nine. The topic you chose was covered in chapter two." Although the case is obviously closed to the professor at this point, and this student might feel angry or unfairly treated, he would do well to hold his tongue and respond with something like, "Oh, I see; I must have missed that in the instructions. Was it written on the assignment?" rather than something aggressive such as, "I feel there's some gray area here; you didn't explain the assignment very well, and besides, what does it really matter what chapter it comes from if everyone is writing about something different anyway?"

In many cases, if you are willing to shoulder some of the responsibility, the professor may come around and add a few points to the grade. The latter response, although it may represent how you feel, is not going to make the professor want to change the grade. In fact, it feels like bullying, and bullying will get you nowhere in academia. We know of one professor who routinely lowers a student's grade if he feels bullied, especially in instances where he has graded that particular assignment lightly as a whole in the first place. Remember, your professor holds the right to *lower* a grade as well as raise it. Similarly, saying that a grade is causing you to lose your scholarship or will disqualify you from entering the graduate program you already have been accepted to may be seen as "guilt tripping" by the professor. Trying to guilt a professor into changing your grade is unethical and will not produce the results you are looking for; you might even end up with a lower grade.

Challenging a final course grade and getting results is even trickier. At most universities, professors have to fill out paperwork giving a plausible explanation as to why we are changing the grade and have it approved and signed by both the department chairperson and the dean, both of whom have the right to deny the request. You can understand why an explanation such as "the student came to see me and explained that she tried harder in this class than in any other she's ever taken," or, "the student says that this grade will cause her to lose her eligibility to play volleyball" will be denied by the dean. You must give the professor hard evidence as to why the grade should be changed, otherwise, the professor's hands are tied.

Changing a final course grade also means extra work for the professor after the end of a term. When a term is over, most professors are no longer on contract and are not geared up to attend to teaching-related duties, i.e., over the summer or another break. Always wait until the start of the next term to challenge a course grade, unless you have recently graduated and are about to move on. At the very least, win points for yourself by emailing the professor that you are concerned about your final grade and would like to review it with him or her when school starts again in the fall. This shows that you are respectful of the professor's time and are willing to discuss it rather than to make demands.

If you have a legitimate reason for challenging your grade, but the professor disagrees with your rationale and will not change the grade, you may formally challenge your grade (known as a **grade appeal**). At many universities, a grade appeals committee exists. You may request a hearing with a panel of professors (and sometimes students) who will then be given the ultimate decision regarding the grade. The committee or hearing panel's decision is always final. Before going to such extreme measures, imagine having to make the case for why your grade should be changed to a panel of seasoned professors and to some of your school's best students. If you do not have all of your supporting facts ready, the hearing can quickly devolve into a situation that is embarrassing and ultimately devastating for you. Believe it or not, student representatives on such panels are often harsher than the professors.

How High Are Academic Integrity Expectations?

Academic integrity refers to completing work honestly in college and making a conscious choice to engage in ethical behavior when doing assignments. Since this is an issue of grave importance on campuses nationwide, this topic will be covered in greater depth later. Here, let it suffice to say that academic integrity standards are much higher at the university level than at the secondary school level. Colleges and universities espouse conduct guidelines that forbid cheating, and they take these codes very seriously. Sometimes, these codes are called **honor codes**. You may be asked to read your college's honor code during orientation and to sign your name saying that you pledge to uphold its terms. Be aware that every professor has dealt with cheating and that colleges can, and do, expel students who are caught acting dishonestly.

Glossary

Academic integrity—making the conscious choice to employ ethical behavior when completing assignments in college.

Chairperson—the individual who heads an entire academic department (also known as a department head).

Challenge—in academia, to cause one to work at and above their intellectual comfort level.

Cram/Cramming—see *mass repetition studying*.

Dean—the individual who oversees an entire school within a university.

Distributed repetition studying—rehearsing and apportioning exam study material over several weeks.

Extracurricular activities—college-sponsored activities (service, clubs, sports) that are not a required part of the academic curriculum.

FERPA—Family Educational Rights and Privacy Act; the government act restricting nonauthorized access to student academic records.

Grade appeal—when a student challenges a grade; a hearing is convened to hear both sides of the story and to decide on the final grade.

Honor code—a school's code of behavior for promoting honesty and discouraging cheating.

Information literacy—understanding how to find and use information.

Journal article—a written publication, shorter than a book, that argues a specific point or presents new, original research; published in a periodically occurring academic print or online magazine.

Mass repetition studying—rehearsing exam study material during a single study period or over a short time period; also known as cramming.

Matriculate—to begin college or be admitted to a university

Office hours—the available times a professor sets aside specifically for meeting with students.

Primary source—in writing and research, the original source of information.

Rote memorization—the continuous and mechanical rehearsal of study material.

Secondary source—in writing and research, sources using information obtained from **primary sources.**

Syllabus—an instructor's preterm summary document listing how to contact the instructor, the course requirements, the course schedule, and other information needed to succeed in the course.

Term—the period of time designated by a college or university system that marks the beginning and end of a set of courses. For some colleges/universities, this is a semester and for others this might be quarters.

Textbook schema—one's knowledge or concept of the kinds of information a textbook contains.

What Am I Expected to Know about How College Works?

2

Just as in a work setting, where it is important to understand the business structure and its staff, you will maneuver more efficiently within the university system if you understand how it operates. For example, you might have to obtain a signature from a department head in order to drop a class. In this situation, you will obviously have to know what a department head is. Here, we will describe the typical college or university hierarchy, starting from the top.

Who Can Help Me?
FINDING THE APPROPRIATE HELP

Different colleges and universities have different kinds of structures, but there are some common ones. The university president (on some campuses, the provost or chancellor, although some institutions have both) oversees the complete operation of the university. He or she secures money for the university and decides, through consultation, how the money will be spent. Parents sometimes contact the president's office when they are unhappy with their student's grades or with their student's dorm situation. These parents might be surprised to learn that these types of complaints are not handled within this office. Contacting the president is not like contacting a school principal; these complaints will be transferred to one of the following university positions.

At some schools, a vice president (sometimes also called the dean of faculties, academic dean, or provost) helps oversee university affairs and acts as the supervisor of all the professors. In other words, he or she handles faculty and academic issues.

Other administrators and their areas might include a vice president for student affairs (sometimes

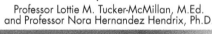

Professor Lottie M. Tucker-McMillan, M.Ed. and Professor Nora Hernandez Hendrix, Ph.D.

Image courtesy of Miami Dade College - North Campus

Table 2.1 Who do I call? Common student issues and the appropriate contact

Person or Office	Issue
Professor or Instructor	• Questions about course grades, grading, assignments, class, requirements for the major
Department Chairperson/Head or Department Office	• Concerns about professor/instructor behavior • Questions about requirements for the major • Reporting instances of cheating • Questions about credit transfer for classes taught in this department • Applications and paperwork related to the major
School or College Dean or Office	• Concerns about department chairperson/head • Concerns about professor/instructor not addressed at department level
Dean of Students Student Affairs Office	• Reporting harassment (students or personnel) • Concerns about university housing • Concern about a fellow student (potential to harm self or others—immediate threats should be reported to campus police) • Information about campus resources • Reporting personal emergencies that interfere with one's ability to continue classes • Roommate issues
Registrar's Office	• Questions about registration, student records, transcripts, graduation, transferring, university catalog
Campus Housing Student Housing	• Questions about campus living, meal plans, roommates, campus activities
Bursar/Campus Business Office	• Questions about tuition, fees, bills, payments, loans, scholarships, grants

called a dean of students); a vice president for business and finance; a vice president for enrollment management; and a vice president for university advancement. Of these individuals, the one who affects you most directly is the dean of students. This is the person who keeps track of student problems (e.g., cheating, arrest, death in the family, illness). If you have a problem, it may ultimately be resolved in this dean's office.

Universities are typically divided into separate divisions or schools (or "colleges" in some institutions) such as the school of liberal arts, school of science (these two are often combined in smaller universities), school of engineering, school of law, school of education, school of business, school of fine arts, and school of health sciences.

Individual departments are housed in these schools. For example, the English department will be located in the school of liberal arts, the civil engineering department in the school of engineering.

At the head of each school is a dean. This person oversees all of the departments within a school/college unit. A chairperson (or department head) directs each academic department.

How Do I Get the Chairperson's Signature?
HOW ACADEMIC DEPARTMENTS CAN HELP YOU

Academic departments represent intellectual divisions of an entire academic discipline (e.g., chemistry, theater, accounting, electrical engineering). Each department has a specified campus location and comprises a head (or chairperson), full-time tenured or tenure-track faculty members, and a rotating group of part-time instructors. Knowledgeable administrative assistants or secretaries usually support the faculty. Departments may be physically housed in an entire building (as is the case at large universities) or in a subsection of one floor of a building at smaller universities. Each department typically has a main office where you will find the secretary (who can usually answer most of your major-related questions and can certainly direct you to the appropriate paperwork or university office if needed), the head or chairperson of the department (the person overseeing the operation of the department and its staff), and information about the major. Most also have a departmental website where you can learn more about the degrees or programs the department offers and the faculty who teach in the department. In general, faculty offices are usually located in or near the appropriate department, but do not be surprised if **lecturers** (part-time instructors, also called **adjunct professors**) do not have their own offices or if their offices are located outside the department.

Professor Lottie M. Tucker-McMillan

Image courtesy of Miami Dade College - North Campus

All faculty members are dedicated teachers (smaller universities) or researchers (larger universities) or a combination of both (medium-sized universities). Each one of us has a special area of focus within our discipline. For example, a history professor might specialize in the plight of women in ancient Greece, or an art professor might specialize in ceramic sculpture. Faculty enjoy talking about their academic passion, so feel free to approach them and ask them more about what they do and why they do it.

Can I Really Talk to My Professors?
LEARNING TO APPROACH FACULTY MEMBERS

It is important to notice that professors have unique titles and degrees. These distinctions are significant within the university system. Academic titles include professor emeritus, (full) professor, associate professor, assistant professor, temporary assistant professor, instructor (also called lecturer or adjunct professor), and graduate assistant. The more you understand about these titles and degrees, the better chance you will have of knowing how to gain the faculty's favor.

What do the titles mean? To understand the answer to this question, you must first be familiar with the notion of **tenure**. Tenure in the academic system is defined as permanent-employee status. You might hear of a faculty member "getting tenure." This means that the faculty member has worked for many years to make a rigorous cut and has become a permanent member of his or her department and of the university. His or her employment cannot be terminated without due process. As you might expect, this is a very comfortable and coveted position. Imagine joining a company and never worrying about layoffs or getting fired.

Faculty members work hard to acquire tenure. In fact, it is often the most difficult step in a professor's career. The faculty member works for years to meet very specific and rigorous requirements that include peer review, **student evaluations** (student assessments of a professor's teaching), research, university service, academic service, academic development, and publication. Despite the term, it does not take ten years to acquire tenure. In fact, faculty members usually apply for tenure during their fourth, fifth, or sixth year at the university. Most are required to apply by their seventh year at the latest. Some faculty members, despite having worked extremely hard, fail to receive tenure. When this is the case, they are let go and must seek employment elsewhere. The **American Association of University Professors** (AAUP) closely guards the tenure system, which is the watchdog group for professors.

What Do I Need to Know about Professors' Titles?

Back to the original question: What are academic titles, and what do they mean? We will start from the bottom, in terms of pay and prestige, and will work our way to the top of the hierarchy.

Table 2 Professors' Titles and Their Meaning

Title	Meaning
Graduate Instructor (Teaching Assistant)	• a graduate student in the area of study he or she is assigned to teach • may have earned a master's degree, although many only have baccalaureate, or undergraduate, degrees, but are far along in their course of study and prepared to assist at the undergraduate level • unranked, but close to the professors
Lecturer (Adjunct Professor)	• teaches part time • does not necessarily have a doctoral degree, but most have master's degrees • not eligible to apply for tenure; works on a contract that may or may not be renewed each term or year • usually not required to engage in any university activity beyond teaching • unranked
Temporary Assistant Professor (Term Professor)	• faculty member hired to teach full time • position is not tenure track; contract may be periodically renewed, but usually not more than once or twice • might be expected to engage in other activities beyond teaching, such as scholarship, departmental committees, and university service • unranked
Assistant Professor	• hired full time, considered tenure track or tenure stream (someone who does not have tenure but who is eligible to apply for it in their fourth, fifth, or sixth year) • position will become permanent only if tenure is achieved • offered beginning rank, but must prove self to chairperson, associate, and full professor colleagues
Associate Professor	• has been promoted from the assistant professor level (comes with pay raise) • generally paired with getting tenure • along with full professors, recommends whether an assistant professor is worthy of tenure • intermediate rank

(continued)

Table 2 Professors' Titles and Their Meaning (*continued*)

Title	Meaning
Professor or Full Professor	• when capitalized as a title, this is another promotion (up from the associate level), accompanied by another pay raise • has typically worked in their department for at least ten years, unless hired at full level • promotion to this level is extremely difficult, usually requires international recognition and a lengthy publication record • some professors never reach this level • along with associate professors, recommends whether an assistant professor is worthy of tenure • highest rank
Professor Emeritus	• title conferred on someone whose entire career contributions have been exceptionally meritorious • title conferred around the time that the professor retires from the university • sometimes granted option to maintain ties with the department (can teach a class, keep office) • not all universities offer this title • most admired by colleagues

What Kind of Degrees Do My Professors Have?

Just as with academic titles, it is important to understand the various degrees that professors might have. As you will learn, not all disciplines offer the doctorate and so some full professors may not be called "doctor."

Table 3 Advanced Degrees and Their Meaning

Advanced Degree	Meaning
MA (master of arts) MS (master of science) MFA (master of fine arts) MBA (master of business administration)	• earned after bachelor's degree • requires at least two years of graduate study • most of the humanities offer MA degrees, most sciences offer MS degrees • MFA is an advanced degree for the fine arts and creative writing that is the highest degree for those disciplines • not usually qualified to obtain a tenure-track professor position at a major university (MFA is exception)

(*continued*)

Table 3 Advanced Degrees and Their Meaning (*continued*)

Advanced Degree	Meaning
PharmD (doctor of pharmacy) JD (doctor of jurisprudence) MD (doctor of medicine) DO (doctor of osteopathy) PsyD (doctor of psychology)	• are professional degrees • practicing pharmacists earn the first listed degree, the second is for lawyers or attorneys, and the latter are for practicing physicians or psychologists • PharmD is a four-year degree that follows the first two years of undergraduate coursework • **JD** degree typically requires three years of post-baccalaureate study • MD requires four years plus a residency of approximately three years • PsyD requires five years including an **internship** (an unpaid supervised work position used to gain specific work experience or specialized training) • **MD** and **PsyD** are called doctor, those with a JD are not; the PharmD is less clear—some might be called doctor, but the practice appears to have some controversy
EdD (doctor of education)	• sometimes considered a research degree, sometimes a professional degree • can teach and conduct research at the university level, but often works as a professional in a school system • has a more applied focus; the PhD is more research based • requires about four years of study
PhD (doctor of philosophy)	• is a research degree • can teach at the highest academic levels and conduct original research in their disciplines • can obtain a PhD in almost any discipline, even medicine (in order to conduct medical research) • is not a doctorate in the field of philosophy (it is a degree that denotes that the individual understands and can teach the philosophical underpinnings of their specific discipline) • considered the highest academic degree, qualifies individual to obtain a tenure-track position at any university level • can take four to ten years given the amount of work needed to complete a **dissertation** (an original work of research considered to be the culmination of one's study) • person referred to as doctor

How Do I Get to Know My Professors?

Students have two common complaints about their professors. First, professors are intimidating simply by virtue of their status and expertise level. Second, professors are not very accessible. Admittedly, sometimes professors just do not seem approachable, and they can seem gone all the time. However, you do want to get to know some of your professors because they can later boost your career by acting as a mentor or serving as a job reference. Of course, this means you will have to find them first and then get past the intimidation factor. Here, we explain why professors may sometimes seem to be missing in action and also provide tips for breaking the ice.

Where Is My Professor?

Those outside academia are often surprised to learn that teaching is only one component of a professor's job. We are actually required to engage in a number of non-teaching activities as part of our job. Generally, the three major facets of a professor's job include teaching, research, and service.

Could be teaching, advising, or preparing. We spend quite a bit of time preparing for the classes we teach. This involves writing lectures, creating assignments and tests, preparing handouts/overhead/PowerPoint presentations, maintaining a class website, and keeping abreast of the latest research on the course topic by reading articles, books, journals, and interacting with peers. We grade your work (something we take very seriously) and meet with our academic advisees (students majoring in our academic area). We also write letters of recommendation for scholarships, internships, jobs, and graduate programs, and, sometimes, advise student club meetings.

Could be doing research. This can be anything from observing infants to gain an understanding of their cognitive abilities, to mapping the geography of Mars, to unearthing the remains of an ancient Greek temple. Research involves spending a good deal of our time reading the latest information in our field, collecting information, developing research questions, and designing research studies. We attend conferences. We write articles, books, or textbooks. We choreograph dances or exhibit paintings. We write grant proposals to request monetary support for our research activities. Our research takes place during the academic year, during summers and holidays, and sometimes while on **sabbatical** (a paid term or year away from campus specifically for research).

Could be engaged in service. On campus, service entails participating in committee work, heading organizations or institutes, attending meetings, and writing reports related to these activities. Off-campus service might include accounting professors preparing taxes for underprivileged citizens, counseling professors offering free support groups, law school professors providing free legal advice, or even art professors painting a mural for a public building. On the national level, a faculty member might act as an officer for a professional organization such as the American Chemical Association, the American Psychological Association, the Modern Languages Association, or the College Art Association.

When you cannot find us, we are probably engaged in one of these three types of activities and are most likely not available. However, do not let this deter you. You should get to know your professors. Try sending us an email, writing us a *formal* letter, or stopping by during our posted office hours. You can even set up an appointment with the department secretary. Though we seem to run by you as we move from duty to duty, do know that we would love to talk with you about what we do.

Are Professors Intimidating?

We will not lie to you; some professors are very intimidating (even to us, and we are their colleagues!). Others only seem intimidating but are actually very friendly. Do not rely on gender or other visual cues (type of dress) to guide your decision. Women professors are not necessarily going to be more caring, and the professor with the edgy clothing is not necessarily interested in students. You will just need to learn who is who and rely on the fact that most professors are nice people. If you are interested in a particular subject area or in getting to know a specific professor, just give it a try. The worst that could happen is that the professor does not have time for you. Some people are just not friendly that way. Move on to someone else. If you never try, you could be missing out on a wonderful lifelong mentor.

Schedule some time to meet with us or accompany us to lunch. Use this time to ask us questions about our life and work. Believe it or not, this is really easy because professors love to talk about themselves (or at least their work). Use the information on what we do to conquer feelings of intimidation and break the ice with your professor. Now that you have a sense of our work duties, you might ask "Why do you teach the courses you teach?, Why did you choose this topic?, What do you enjoy about teaching?, Can you tell me about your current research project?, How did you choose your field?, What else do you do at this university?, How did you end up at this university?, What were you like as a student?, What committees are you on?, What conferences are you attending this year?, …" Of course, you do not want to simply pepper us with disingenuous questions. Just start a conversation and see where it leads you. Sometimes, when we do all the talking and you all the listening, we develop a really positive impression of you.

Professor Lottie M. Tucker-McMillan

Image courtesy of Miami Dade College - North Campus

The time we commit to all of our activities and to the quality of our work are extremely important to us. We cannot earn **tenure** (permanent employee status) or promotion unless we prove our genuine dedication to you, our students, and to our department, our universities, and our disciplines. Furthermore, the work we do beyond the university enhances the reputation of your university. Now you know who we are. However, you are also a part of the university structure—the most important part.

Glossary

Academic departments—intellectual divisions of an entire academic discipline that have a designated campus location.

Adjunct professor—an individual who teaches a university course on a part-time basis (also called a **lecturer**).

American Association of University Professors (AAUP)—the watchdog group for professors who, among other things, defends the concept of tenure, insists on shared rather than top-down governance within universities, and censures universities who do not uphold best practices.

Lecturer—an individual who teaches a university course on a part-time basis only (also called an adjunct)

Sabbatical—when a college or university gives a faculty member paid time off from teaching (usually a term or year) to focus on research.

Student evaluations—student classroom assessments of a professor's teaching.

Tenure—permanent-employee status granted by universities to professors if they have fulfilled a set of rigorous research and teaching requirements within a set time period.

What Will Be Expected of Me as a College Student?

3

You have worked hard to get into college and we realize this. We also know that for the traditional student, transitioning from high school to college is not always easy. You may feel torn between the roles of dependent adolescent (your permanent address is still with your family, your family may help pay for your education/car/insurance, you may feel the need to go home on weekends or during the summer) and independent adult (your schedule is up to you, no one is monitoring you or how you spend your time, you are completely responsible for your grades and class work). There are also many habits and practices that you may have picked up in high school (or were even taught) that you will find are not acceptable in college. In essence, you will need to learn a new system of conduct.

You already know that this transition period is not available to everyone. Many people simply become an adult by virtue of having children, getting a job right away, or moving out of their parents' house. In other words, they did not have the option of a transition period. You worked hard to get here, so do not drop the ball. Use your resources to learn this new system and to maneuver through it successfully.

Campuses provide many resources for you. Learn what they are and how to use them. This handbook is one resource. Follow this guidance and you will be one step ahead of your peers. Universities and your professors are committed to getting you through this transition period. Our duty is to help shape you into mature, knowledgeable, and articulate adults. While you may question the value of many of the readings and assignments you are given and the classes you must take, you must trust that they serve a purpose in

Image courtesy of Miami Dade College - North Campus

Professor Ginny Peterson-Tennant, Ph.D.

preparing you for the world after college. How you conduct yourself today will affect the way you perform in the workforce and in your personal life.

One of the most important skills that college helps you develop is associating with others. Through student activities, living with roommates (if you have the opportunity), and group projects, you will learn how to interact with your peers. However, it is also important that you learn how to relate to your superiors. The savvy student understands that he or she should conduct him or herself one way with friends and differently with professors or supervisors.

Why Shouldn't I Call Her Ms.?
HOW TO ADDRESS INSTRUCTORS

Professors do what they do because they love their academic fields and want to share what they know with you and others. It is rare to find the professor who does not do many things for the university and the community for free. They deserve your respect, even if you dislike them, disagree with their policies, or are earning a lower grade than you would like. You will encounter many people throughout your life, not just in college, who also deserve your respect.

Someone with a doctoral degree (PhD, PsyD, EdD, MD) should always be addressed as "Dr. So-and-So." The generic "Professor" So-and-So" is also acceptable. When in doubt, you may use "professor," without even adding the last name. This simple form of address is especially helpful if it is difficult to pronounce your instructor's name. In general, it is not proper form to call anyone with a doctoral degree by their first name, unless they invite you to do so. Likewise, calling an instructor Mr., Mrs., Ms., or Miss is not proper. Although you probably did so in high school, it is a practice you should cease in college. Be especially mindful to refrain from calling female professors Mrs., Ms., or Miss. There is some sensitivity involved in this issue because many students continue to call their female professors "Ms." while referring to their male counterparts as "Dr.," even if the male professor does not possess a doctoral degree. This misusage implies that one gender is deserving of the title but the other is not. If calling your instructor "professor," or even "doctor," feels awkward to you at first, practice at home. Try saying the following out loud: "Professor, when may I stop by your office for extra help?" or "Dr. Harris, is a paper on ornithology appropriate for this assignment?" Once you know the correct title to use, be sure to apply it not only when speaking to your professor but in all written or email correspondence.

You will eventually want to err on the side of caution when addressing superiors in the workplace as well. The use of "doctor" is less common in industry, but you can use your new skill of assessing cultural norms to determine how to address your colleagues.

Just as with universities, companies vary in interpersonal culture depending on their location and the type of industry.

What Do I Say to My Professor?
HANDLING MEETINGS WITH INSTRUCTORS

Be prepared when you meet with your academic advisor or with a professor, and do not miss these meetings. We know of at least one faculty member who will drop you as an advisee if you miss a meeting. This is regarded as entirely fair, because professors are busy and often have to make special accommodations (like canceling other meetings, delaying work on research, or even skipping meals) in order to meet with you. In general, be mindful of the fact that professors have many other duties besides teaching and interacting with students, and they are chronically pressed for time. Here are some tips.

Do . . .

- Consult the course syllabus for the professor's listed office hours.

- Politely request a meeting. It is up to the professor when you meet, so you may need to be flexible.

- Notify the professor ahead of time (ideally, at least one day ahead) if you need to reschedule the meeting.

- Come prepared with notes and questions.

- Take notes or at least write down future meeting times and dates. Writing things down during meetings shows an awareness of meta-memory—an understanding of the limits of one's memory. Even if you think you will remember what is said, write it down anyway. It is a good habit to develop in college.

- Be respectful during the meeting. Turn your cell phone *completely off* before entering the office.

- Show judgment in what you say and reveal to your professor. Remember, everything you say is being evaluated.

Do Not . . .

- Miss a meeting with a faculty member.

- Check your phone if it rings, vibrates, or receives a text message.

- Answer your phone. Some professors will end the meeting right then.

► Make comments that reveal a lack of commitment to school or inappropriate priorities, such as the following:

- "Is this an easy class?/Is this professor easy?" This statement says to us that you are unwilling to challenge yourself. In addition, it is not our place (nor is it ethical) for us to discuss a colleague's questionable teaching skills with you. This is a better question for your friends or classmates.

- "I hate statistics/math/science." These are important courses to many areas of study. For example, statistics is an integral part of psychology and business, and its mastery is absolutely necessary if you plan on getting a job in the field or attending graduate school.

- "I'm not good at math." Few are, but you get better at it by doing it, not avoiding it. Try to demonstrate your tenacity by saying instead, "I've never done well in math, but I am willing to try. What resources on campus might help me with this course?"

- "I only want to take classes on Tuesdays and Thursdays," or "only Mondays, Wednesdays, and Fridays," or "I don't want any Friday classes," or "I don't want any morning classes; I'm not good in the morning." This simply shows a lack of dedication to school. In order to graduate on time, you will have to take what you can get. Obviously, some personal commitments may partially dictate your schedule (sports team practice, work-study obligations), but know that you will have to be flexible in your selection of courses.

- "I chose my courses based on the online grade distributions for the courses" or "based on the reviews at ratemyprofessor.com." We do not think these sources reliably convey helpful information about a course or an instructor. After all, anybody can post ratings online, including professors themselves. Although you might think this statement shows you have done some background research, we interpret this as evidence that you are after the grade rather than the information.

- "I think Professor So-and-So is hot." This is not the kind of comment your instructors can or should acknowledge. It is also poor judgment to say this to a professor. Remarks like this should stay within your peer group.

heyyyy you! did i miss anything important?
PRACTICING PROFESSIONAL COMMUNICATION SKILLS

"So, I was like, and then she was like, it was like, you know, like what was that?" This is not the type of speech you should be using in college. Unfortunately, it is a hard habit to break (admittedly, you might hear faculty members picking up trendy words and phrases, too). Such speech, however, will only make you sound immature. Begin the practice of dropping the words *like* and *you know* when talking in class, and then weed out other trendy terms and phrases. A warning: Because trendy speech habits are hard to break, you might find yourself using them in class or—gulp—in an interview. Does it really matter that much? Absolutely. One of us sat on a university committee that interviews students for a prestigious business mentorship program. She noticed that a few of these students, who are top university students with stellar grades and **résumés** (a self-prepared professional document summarizing one's schooling and work experiences), frequently used the word *like* in their speech during the interview. These students were automatically placed in the "no" pile. Based on the use of *like* in their speech alone they lost the chance to compete for the position. Why? Students in this position were going to meet with **chief executive officers** (CEOs, the highest managerial position in a company) of top businesses. They needed to be able to converse seriously with important individuals, and candidates needed to reflect well on the university. How do you think these CEOs would react to this kind of speech?

No matter how quick or casual the message, always use clear and appropriate language. This includes emails and other written correspondence with professors. After all, one trait of the college-educated individual is being an excellent—not a so-so—writer. Writing-intensive experiences exist throughout the curriculum for this reason. Many professors refuse to reply to students who cannot craft a properly written email (for example: "I left class early 2day what did i miss do i need to bring anything on monday"). Be aware that higher-paying jobs require that you communicate in writing with no spelling, punctuation, or grammar errors.

Please do not email your professor unless it is important; ask any quick questions after class or during office hours. Follow the same rules for email as you would for a class assignment; use language that is respectful and clear. Do not use cute salutations such as, "hey Dr. Jane!" or subject lines like, "I'm GOING CRAZY." Every email message you send should include a reference to who you are and in exactly which class (days and time) you are enrolled. Professors often teach multiple sections of the same course, so simply writing that you are in, for instance, "our Spanish class" is not clear enough. Use standard grammatical and punctuation rules, including capital letters.

Avoid sending emails like these examples:

Donna, I dropped by to see u today but u were in your research lab. when r your office hours because i need to c u

heyyy you! what did i miss in class today? i was sick as a Dog

> Doctor S., will you tell me what my grade on the first exam was because i cant remember

Here is an example of an effective email (note the excellent writing and respectful tone):

> Dear Professor Milledge,
>
> Yesterday in class, I was interested in the portion of your lecture on new criminal behaviors—the part on Internet crimes. When the class has finished reading the book you put on reserve in the library on this topic, would you mind taking it off reserve so that my study partner, Skye Simon, or I could check it out and take it home? If this is a problem, we understand. Please let me know. Thanks.
>
> Maria Hidalgo (Criminology 210/MWF 9:00-9:50)

Can I Leave My Bag in Your Office?
RESPECTING BOUNDARIES

Observe office hours. It is important to respect a professional's office hours. These are hours set aside specifically for students or visitors.

> ▸ *A professor's office hours.* You can find office hours listed on the syllabus, the office door, or in the department office. This is when you should stop by to ask questions about class material, to retrieve graded work, or to just chat. Due to changing class schedules, professors set new office hours each term. If classes are not in session (for example, during exams, holidays, and breaks), there are no office hours. So if you want to discuss your end-of-the-term grade, plan on doing it the next term. When set office hours conflict with your class times, make a specific appointment through email or after class.

> ▸ *University offices hours.* Most offices observe business hours. That is, opening at 8 A.M. and closing at 5 P.M. Staff usually take a lunch hour around noon. Sometimes, staff sit in the office to eat lunch. You might even see them sitting in there behind a locked door. Even though you can see them, please do not bother them during this time; it could be their only break of the day. Come back later when the office is open.

Respect office space and equipment. It is important to get into the habit of respecting office space. Business leaders have complained that new undergraduate hires do not know how to interact with bosses or how to respect space. Treat faculty and staff member offices as you would any business superior's office. Practice being respectful

My Professor Was Crabby When I Stopped By!

Did you show up outside of office hours? This is not always a good idea, even if you see our door open or if we are cheerful and spend time with you. Often, we need to be able to make phone calls, work on our computers, and confer with colleagues uninterrupted. Even quick questions can get us off task, especially if we are in the middle of writing. If our mind is on other matters, it is difficult to shift our focus. Please make an effort to see us during office hours so that we can work with you when our minds are clear and we are focused on your concerns. You deserve our undivided attention!

with university space and this proper behavior will automatically transfer to your future work life.

- *The office.* Do not enter a private office without first being invited. If you knock on the office door and there is no answer, please do not rattle the doorknob. There is no answer either because no one is there or because the professor is busy and does not want to be disturbed. An unlocked door is not an invitation to enter. You should never open a closed office door.

- *The equipment.* Do not use a professional's computer or stand behind a professional and read what is on the computer screen (unless first invited). Professional offices contain valuable equipment, important documents, and confidential information. Professors keep research records, exams, grades, and other student information in their offices. We often have confidential information on our computers (e.g., a student's transcript) or need to input confidential information (such as our ID and password on the university computer system).

- *Borrowing equipment.* Do not ask faculty and staff to borrow items such as telephones, staplers, computers, printers, etc. Borrowing items sends the message that you are unprepared, completing an assignment at the last minute, lazy, or just disrespectful. Learning to be self-sufficient is important preparation for the business world.

Respect private time. A professional should never be contacted at home or on a cell phone unless permission has been given to do so. Questions about grades, exams,

My Professor Is Out of the Office, and I Really Need to Drop Off This Paper!

Entering a closed office because you want to leave an assignment in there is not acceptable. All faculty members have mailboxes located in their department's main office where students can leave assignments. Or you can leave assignments with the office secretary. Occasionally, a professor will have a box on his or her office door where you can leave any correspondence or work. Please, avoid sliding your paper under the door where it may be stepped on.

assignments, recommendation letters, and other similar items are best reserved for office hours.

▶ *During school breaks.* Avoid contacting professors over the summer and during breaks (unless you are taking a class from that professor during that time period). Questions about what books to purchase for next term and other non-emergency topics should wait until the new term starts. If you have questions about your final grade, or want to dispute a grade, wait until the start of the next term when professors are in their offices and can review all of your work.

▶ *Emergencies.* Learn to identify the difference between a temporarily stressful situation (e.g., not knowing what to study and the exam is scheduled for the next day) and an emergency (e.g., a life-and-death situation). In a class-related stressful situation, practice finding a way to solve the problem on your own. In the case of a true emergency, your professor is really not the appropriate contact person. Contact the following entities in true emergencies:

- Contact Campus/Local Police or 911: suicide threats; suspicious persons; weapons on campus; overdoses; serious accidents; threats of harm

- Contact the Dean of Students Office: unexpected death of a loved one; automobile accident requiring hospitalization; severe illness requiring extended hospitalization or care; unexpected act of nature that causes extreme disruption (e.g., house fire, tornado, hurricane)

What's Wrong with Facebooking in Class?
GOOD USE OF SOCIAL NETWORKING AND CLASSROOM TECHNOLOGY

You may be allowed to use your personal laptop or tablet to take notes, to work on a project, or to complete an activity. Most professors are supportive of this, but they also have specific policies regarding their use. Read the course syllabus for policies that apply to specific classes. In general, your use of technology in the classroom should not interfere with class learning. Turn off the sound (including the power-on and off "music"). Also pay attention to how much sound your keyboard typing makes.

Surfing the web or reading email during class will interfere with your learning. Two pitfalls arise from engaging in nonclass-related computer or phone activity. The first is that when you try to multitask (take notes and surf/check email at the same time) you miss class information. You can only truly attend to one thing at a time, especially if it is new information like lecture material. You also distract other students. Unfortunately, it is becoming increasingly difficult to regulate classroom web use without interrupting the flow of the class. Please sit at the back of the class if you know you will use your computer to web surf or check email. How does your computer use distract other students, even if they cannot see the entire computer screen? When you shift from page to page, the light and color of the screen changes and flickers, and students around you become restless and annoyed. Sitting at the back ensures that fellow students will be less disturbed. Practice polite classroom technology use, and many instructors will happily allow you to continue.

Social networking is ubiquitous on college campuses. Students spend many, many hours on social networking sites—too many, in some cases. While being technologically proficient is a great skill, we have to warn that social media has its dangers. Everything you post (your pictures, personal information) may be seen by more than just your friends and peers. The university dean of students, police, internship coordinators, and company recruiters often troll social media websites. These people are looking for party postings (ever wonder how the cops know where the parties are located?) and inappropriate behaviors. Are you younger than 21 and did you post a picture of yourself drinking beer at a party? If so, the local police might be taking note. Are there other unprofessional pictures of you posted? If so, employers might notice. Employers, including internship coordinators, are known to weed out applicants based on Facebook postings. Do not assume they are just looking at your pictures. What you write about yourself is also important. Unfortunately, employers might even weed you out based on your religious affiliation, political leanings, or other beliefs. Is this legal? No, but no one will ever know that is the reason you never received an interview.

We recently heard a story of a student who naively posted select lyrics to a rap song on a friend's Facebook page. The lyrics made reference to wanting to blow up the school. This student was subsequently arrested and held in jail for almost a week. He was charged with making terrorist threats—a felony charge. Even if he did not mean to make such threats or thought the post would be funny, the authorities had to treat his act seriously—and they did. Now this young man has a felony charge on his record for the rest of his life, which he will have to report on every job application. It is a big price to pay for one very bad decision. Be careful about your public behavior now that you are considered an adult.

One last point about Facebook is that you do not want to extend an offer to a professor to be your friend on this site. This is inappropriate and could be seen as a lack of understanding, on your part, of the professional relationship that must exist between students and faculty. A good rule of thumb is to not friend your superiors unless they have made it explicit that doing so is okay with them.

Do I Really Have to Be on Time?
PRACTICING COURSE AND CLASSROOM ETIQUETTE

In the classroom, your behavior is just as important as your work. Pay special attention to both. Just as employers admit to making a judgment about potential employees within the first couple of minutes of an interview, professors also draw conclusions about you as a person based on their brief interactions with you in the classroom. Why does this matter? Consider the following examples.

Professor Ginny Peterson-Tennant, Ph.D.

Image courtesy of Miami Dade College - North Campus

What Is Appropriate Class Behavior?

You already know that there are some obvious behaviors that we discourage, such as lateness, skipping class, using cell phones in class, leaving class early, and distracting whispering. However, professors also notice the smaller behaviors like how you dress, rolling your eyes, slumping in your seats, openly yawning, packing up early, and sitting with your arms crossed. Why should this matter to you? As explained, professors make quick judgments about you based on your classroom behavior, usually unintentionally. When you graduate, you will probably have to ask your professors to write you a letter of recommendation or act as a reference. Professors can give you an excellent recommendation or reference only if you have made a good impression. If you have been a habitually tardy student who skipped class and packed up early, your professor will not endorse you as a potentially good employee. Unfortunately, annoying behavior will stand out more than good behavior, so try to have consistently good behavior. Here are some simple rules to follow.

Using the Syllabus as an Etiquette Guide

Most professors include classroom policies in their syllabus. Always read and adhere to these policies. We understand that they sometimes seem preachy or overly dictatorial, but rest assured that certain points have become policy due to problems others have experienced in the past. They are designed for the problem student, not the typical student. There is also quite a bit of important information on the syllabus that might include how to determine your final grade, whether we allow late assignments, what happens when you miss a test, and the attendance policy. When you have a question regarding classroom etiquette, general policies, or due dates, always consult the syllabus first, not the professor.

Keeping All Graded Assignments

Like everyone else, professors make mistakes. It is possible that a professor will record an incorrect grade or the wrong point total in his or her grade book. As a result, at the end of the term you might receive an inaccurate grade for the course. You have every right to dispute the grade; however, the professor can change the grade only if you can provide evidence that the error was the professor's. Unfortunately, without your graded assignments as proof, you will have no case. Be sure you keep all of your graded assignments in a class folder until you receive the grades for that term. If a professor does not let you keep copies of your exams, write down the grade in this folder. Do not skip the class when you will be going over or receiving your graded exam. This might be the only chance to see your grade. Even if the professor posts your grade somewhere, you will not know if there is a mistake if you do not see the actual exam.

Attending Class

Do not skip any classes. This is the most important advice we can give you. You will always miss important material if you miss even *one* class. There is limited time in the classroom, and professors are very particular about the material that is covered during class time. All of it is important. That is, it is all material that we think you need to know—whether or not it ends up on an exam.

In general, you need to know that each professor has a unique attendance policy. Most professors allow a certain number of absences for any reason (illness, jury duty, a day at the beach—it does not matter) and then cut the grade when a student goes over this number, no matter what the circumstances—even if every absence is a legitimate one. Be aware that some professors allow no absences whatsoever. Some, on the other hand, do not even take roll. You must be responsible enough to make yourself aware of all of the attendance policies you are dealing with in a given term and adhere to them.

If your professors allow a certain number of absences, do not use them for trivial matters. Save excused absences for the inevitable illnesses and emergencies you will encounter. That is why you have been given these absences. Importantly, you must learn the difference between a true emergency and a minor emergency. Professors hear all types of excuses. Remember that professors see the big picture; we weigh your excuse against the countless others we have heard. What seems like an emergency to you may not be an emergency in the larger scope of things. Keep this in mind when you are deciding whether or not you need to skip class (or even tell us why you missed class). Here are some concrete examples of real emergencies vs. trivial matters.

> *Real Emergencies (and how students handled them):*
>   1. Upon moving from one state to another, a student's car caught on fire, and years of thesis work literally went up in smoke. (He still finished his thesis on time.)

2. One student had an emergency appendectomy and missed several classes. However, she returned to class with all of her assignments completed and ready to take her missed quiz.

3. Another student broke her foot, had to use crutches, and had a doctor's excuse to stay off her feet but was still determined to attend class and finish the term. She did.

4. A death in the family or the death of a friend is considered an emergency. Some students needed time off to deal with this tragedy. Others found that continuing with classes and keeping their routines was helpful. You will have to decide which is better for you.

It's True!

One time a professor received a late-night phone call at home from a worried student who was going to miss an exam. This frantic student just found out that her mother, father, and stepfather had all just been killed in a murder-suicide. That the student was concerned about an exam at all under these conditions shows that she was so shaken by her personal circumstances that she was not thinking clearly or rationally. This student would have received the highest of accommodations.

⟩ Trivial Matters

1. A student offered to pick up his friend from the airport and missed class. (Like several excuses on this list, this is the student's choice and is not an emergency.)

2. A student's family scheduled a family trip (or reunion, or vacation, or visit) in the middle of the term, or before the term ended, and asked for special alternate testing dates.

3. Another student scheduled a routine doctor (or dentist) appointment during class and missed class.

4. One student scheduled work hours during class.

5. A student declared that she was late for class because she could not find a parking space.

6. A student missed class because she had stayed up all night taking care of her sick roommate. (This is thoughtful, but she should have taken her roommate to the school infirmary.)

7. A student wanted to reschedule his exam so he could be present at his father's local political campaign fund-raising dinner.

If you must give an excuse, keep it professional. Avoid giving the details of your illness, your family problem, or your bad breakup. "I was absent because I was ill," is enough, or "I will not be in class because I am taking care of a family matter." We cringe when we hear, "I was absent because my brother broke up with his girlfriend, and he was so angry he slammed his fist into the wall and broke it," or "I missed class because I had a yellow crusty rash on my stomach," or, "My three-year-old was vomiting green beans." (You would not believe the excuses we have heard!)

Maturely Handling Absences

If you do miss class, remember that it is your responsibility to find out what you missed. This point, however, warrants clarification. When you have an emergency, by all means take care of yourself first and then contact the professor when you can. However, if you miss class due to a trivial matter, do not expect the professor to re-teach the material. Obtain the notes and any missed assignments from a classmate. If you have questions, visit the professor during office hours. These absence procedures are not unlike the procedures you will have to follow in the workplace. Supervisors do not want to have to stop their own work to give special attention to an employee who took a personal day. It is best to practice these procedures now so that they become second nature in the future.

Staying Seated During Class

Students walk out of class for many reasons, few of which are valid. Examples include to get coffee, talk on the cell phone, or to paint their nails (really!). Any time you get up to leave the room, you make noise or provide a visual distraction. Plus, you find yourself whispering to the person next to you to ask what you missed or to get directions for an assignment that may have been handed out in your absence. This behavior is not only disruptive to the lecturer but also to other students. Show respect for your instructor and classmates by staying seated.

Minding Use of Cell Phones

Another way to show respect for others in the classroom is to get in the habit of keeping your phone turned off during class (and not just on vibrate). Just in case you forget to turn it off, program it with a simple ring or beep. If your telephone does accidentally ring in class, immediately turn it off. Do not check the display to see who is calling or texting. Why not? Because it does not matter; you cannot take the call in class. If checking the display is automatic, consider leaving your phone at home or in your bag. Do not answer your phone or text messages while meeting with your professor. This is disrespectful behavior. Using cell phones outside classrooms and office areas is also disruptive. Avoid talking over personal business or even conducting louder-than-normal conversations with your friends in the hallways. Be mindful of what is going on around you and step outside, or away, from faculty offices to talk.

It is important to practice good cell phone etiquette, because it will matter in the working world. During an interview for a prestigious university program mentioned earlier, a student's cell phone rang, several times. The student knew better than to answer the phone, but the damage was already done. Although she was considered a top candidate for the program, she lost her spot due to the cell phone calls. The committee envisioned the student having lunch with a CEO and having her cell phone ring. It was simply unacceptable. Learn good cell phone etiquette now and your good habits will pay off in the future. Your supervisor will take note.

The Way You Dress Matters

How you dress sends a message about who you are and what type of employee you might be in the future. For the most part, students may wear whatever they want to class. However, you have graduated from a secondary school that placed at least some restrictions on what you could or could not wear. Now that you are an adult, you are expected to go by these general guidelines without being told. Choose your clothes thoughtfully, and remember that you are in class to learn. Do wear clothes that you feel define you as a person and show your individuality. Wearing revealing clothes is not appropriate for the classroom. Save these outfits for life outside the classroom. Likewise, be aware of the meaning of clothing with risqué, rude, or mean-spirited messages, or advertisements, before you wear them. Remember that when you wear this type of item, you support the message or provide that company free advertising. When in doubt, do not wear the item to class. As stated earlier, there are typically no policies on attire, but professors will make mental notes about your ability to make good judgments about what is appropriate in a work setting. Your positive reference letter is at stake. On a more practical note, university buildings, especially at older institutions, are not always known for their superior heating and cooling systems. Be prepared for classrooms that are too cold or too hot.

Being Aware of Body Language

When students roll their eyes, slump in their seats, pack up their belongings early, yawn loudly and openly, and sit with their arms tightly crossed, they convey any or all of the following messages: I don't like this professor; I don't like this class; I am so bored; I already know this stuff; I can't wait to leave; or I'm better than this class. Although these messages may make you look good to your peers, they do not look good to the professor. Likewise, playing up symptoms to make sure your professor notices that you are ill looks like a cry for attention (why did you not stay home?).

What behaviors *do* professors want to see? Students who sit forward in their seats, who ask questions, who nod their heads, who smile, and who wait until the signal before packing up and leaving. We guarantee that if you practice these positive behaviors you will be noticed, and if your final grade is teetering on the edge of a higher grade, it just might be bumped up. Why? You have given the impression that you are interested in the subject, working hard, and enjoying the class. This impression will get you far in college and in business. If acting this way feels unnatural to you at first, keep at it until it feels right. It eventually will. At the very least, this type of behavior will keep you tuned in to what is being said, and you will learn more.

Identifying Special Considerations

If you have a university-documented physical or mental difficulty, please inform your professor at the beginning of the term or at least well before the first assignment and/ or exam. Instructors cannot make special arrangements or give special considerations after the fact. Students with disabilities that will affect their learning should identify themselves during the admissions process. If you did not previously identify yourself but believe that you may need special accommodations for your learning, contact the appropriate university office (the dean of students' office can direct you to the correct office). Usually universities will require special testing before you may claim specific accommodations. Professors who have students with special considerations receive letters describing your situation before class begins and will have detailed instructions on how to help you succeed.

A note of caution for those who do not have a true disability but who want special considerations: In the business world, you probably will not receive any empathy. If something is due in business, it needs to be done without any excuses. College is a good place to practice getting things done without asking for special considerations. Think about what changes you can make in your routine without asking for help. For example, one of the authors used to have a terrible attention problem. It was difficult for her to take exams because she was distracted by other students flipping their test pages, or tapping their pens, or shaking their leg. She realized that the noise was what distracted her, and so she dealt with the situation by wearing earplugs to every exam. Her problem was solved easily and without involving others.

Knowing How to Submit Your Best Work

Like your behavior, the quality of your work conveys information about you as a person. Both professors and employers evaluate you based on your work. But, you already knew this. What you probably did not know is that quality of work involves more than just the substance or content of your writing. It also includes how you present your work. Different professors have different criteria and pet peeves when it comes to submitting assignments, but here are some general rules (some of which may be different from what you learned in high school).

Follow writing guidelines. Professors usually give students specific directions regarding research papers. Guidelines might include a due date, number of pages, number and type of references, margin widths, font type, topic, **APA style** (American Psychological Association, the style used by those in the social sciences) or **MLA style** (Modern Languages Association, the style used by those in the humanities). Usually, specific grade points are assigned to each one of these guidelines. Thus, if you fail to follow any one of them, points will be deducted. We find that a lot of unnecessary points get deducted for failure to follow directions; sometimes this can even be the difference between an A and a B paper. In general, writing differs in each discipline. You learn writing basics in required English classes, and you are taught to apply these skills mainly to the literary arts. Professors are trained to teach you specific, technical, writing skills appropriate to their fields. Learning to write in many styles throughout your college career is a planned aspect of the college experience and is designed to help you develop into a sophisticated, flexible, college-educated writer.

Spelling and grammar always matter. Regardless of the type of class (English, accounting, psychology, chemistry, math), your writing skills will be assessed either directly (grades/

points) or indirectly (professor's general opinion about you as a student and potential employee). Do not ask if spelling or grammar is important. It is always important and it will continue to be important when you get a job. In your future, you will have to write cover letters, résumés, memos, communications, business letters, and notes. In fact, supervisors use spelling and grammar to weed out their job applicants. If you have any typos or any misuses of grammar on your cover letter or résumé, your application may automatically be placed in the "no" pile. You are in college to sharpen these skills, and your professors are here to help you. If you struggle with your writing, you can do four things:

1. always have someone proofread your papers,

2. consult the university writing center,

3. do not avoid writing classes or classes that require writing, and

4. practice, practice, practice. You want to learn how to write while in college, not while on the job.

Submit neat papers. Neatness counts. What constitutes a neat paper in college? A neat paper is typewritten on uniform white paper using black ink; it has a standard font and a font size (10 to 12 point); and it is stapled. It is not okay if your paper is printed with blue ink and has faded lines. Such presentation will say volumes about your inability to produce a professional product. A paper should always state your name, assignment title, class information (professor, course title, and time), and the date. That is all that is needed. A standout student will follow these guidelines even if the assignment does not require them. For example, top students typically type their work even if the assignment is to submit a handwritten journal. These are the students who stand out positively and receive the highest recommendations.

Avoid sloppy work. Sloppy papers are printed on colored paper, are not stapled, have the student's name handwritten in the top corner, and do not follow paper guidelines. You might have learned in high school to fold over the edges of your papers in order to keep them together. This looks sloppy. It shows that you did not take the time to staple your work (and may be that it was completed at the last minute). Buy a stapler. They come in sizes small enough to fit in your backpack, so you will never be caught unprepared.

Avoid decorating your work. Flashy papers might come in fancy plastic covers or folders, contain unnecessary pictures on the front, and use colored ink or nonstandard fonts. Sometimes, students try to make their papers stand out by using showy techniques. Most often this tactic will backfire. Only the *written* part of your paper is graded, unless you are a graphic design major. If you need to include graphs (for instance, for a marketing class), or illustrations (for an art history paper), present these in a clear, straightforward manner without unnecessary decorations. Flashy papers may suggest that you are trying to win extra points to make up for weak content. While a properly prepared paper may look boring to you, trust that it will be well received.

Avoid handwritten work. Sometimes, a professor does not require an assignment to be typed. You will stand out if you type your work anyway. Should you choose to submit handwritten work, be sure it is neat. Do not submit papers that have been ripped out of a notebook with paper pieces hanging off the edges. Avoid using a pen with a flashy ink color (pinks, purples, greens); stick to blue or black ink. Also, take note of your handwriting. Does it look professional? If you are someone who likes to make big circles instead of simply dotting the letter "i" (or worse, dotting your i's with smiley faces or hearts!) you will need to change your style. Professors (and later, supervisors) will view these embellishments as immature.

Choose appropriate assignment topics. On a similar note, the topics you choose for certain kinds of assignments send a message to your professors about your maturity level. While topics are set for some assignments, such as the content for lab reports in the sciences, many assignments in the humanities are open ended. Be aware that what you choose to turn in for open-ended assignments such as journal entries, original plays, or artworks needs to be professional at all times. Even if an assignment involves a personal or self-exploratory component, choose what you write about, or create, carefully. Do not be surprised if your too-personal journal entry handed in for a grade lands you with an appointment with the school counselor. Professors regularly refer students to this office based on attitude, conversations, or information gleaned from class assignments. (We all remember, and want to avoid, tragedies such as those at Columbine, Virginia Tech, and other campuses where troubled students become violent.) When given the chance, avoid turning in work that references drinking, partying, sexual escapades, or other juvenile topics. You can always think of something else to write about.

Being a Good Team Member

Group work is becoming more common at the college level. Acquiring the ability to work well within a group is important because today's workforce depends on people working together to achieve a common goal. Professors purposefully give you group assignments to help you work on this skill. When working in a group as part of a college project, there are several ground rules. These include:

1. making good use of group-work meeting times—that is, keeping on task and keeping general socializing to a minimum;

2. knowing what your particular role or task is within the group and carrying it out; and

3. meeting all deadlines your group establishes, especially if others cannot complete their tasks until you complete yours.

In general, the more organized your group, the better the results (or the grade) you will earn. Consider stepping up to a leadership role if you feel your group has weak members. In general, remember that not only do you depend on others to create a quality final product, but also your group depends on you.

What Do I Do about Awful Teachers, Boring Classes, and Picky Rules?

It is possible that somewhere along your educational journey you will encounter less-than-satisfactory teachers and/or boring classes. For the most part, professors do their best to present material in an interesting way, but students vary in their definitions of "good" teaching. A great class to one student is a terrible class to another; as is reflected in student evaluations. Sometimes, opinions vary so greatly, it is hard to believe the comments are about the same course. Keep in mind that attitude and mind-set are keys to enjoying a class. You have control over these two psychological variables. Unfortunately, you do not have direct control over the class or the professor, but do not despair. There is something to be gained from this experience, and there are ways to subtly influence the professor's behavior.

Consider a terrible teacher and a boring class as training for the future. As an employee, you will at some point be required to attend meetings. These meetings may be long, they may not hold your interest, but they *are* required and *will* help your job performance. Use your time in college to develop a strategy for dealing with these situations. The next time you have a terrible teacher or a boring class, work on changing your own attitude or on trying to find ways to make the situation more palatable. One tactic is to try to ask at least one thoughtful lecture-related question during every class meeting. (For example, "How would this theory apply to... .") Doing so will compel you to listen to the content of the lecture and allow you to look past the delivery. In short, do not avoid the situation or view yourself as a victim; instead, meet the situation head on and take control.

Another way to take charge of a difficult class situation is to keep track of what behaviors and lecture techniques used by the instructor are effective and which ones are ineffective. You can do a couple of things with this information: 1. talk (pleasantly!) with the professor about the class or the lecture style, keeping the conversation about what would help you in particular, and avoiding the appearance that the entire class is ganging up on the instructor. (For instance, "It would help if you would speak more slowly or repeat yourself more until I'm used to your accent, which, by the way, I think is beautiful!"), or (2) report your opinions, at the end of the term, on the student evaluation forms. The next point cannot be stressed enough: Be very concrete with your critiques. Simply writing, "This class sucks," is not going to lead to constructive changes, and it might just turn the instructor into a cynic (you do not want to do this, trust us!). If you have not told instructors *specifically* what is wrong with the class or their teaching style, how can they change it? Professors honestly do not know what makes their class more engaging to you and what does not, so tell them. Writing, "The font on the PowerPoint presentations is too small to read," is very clear and constructive feedback. The instructor knows exactly what to change and will not be upset because there is no angry tone to your comment. Also, be sure to include comments about what the instructor does right. Praise is always effective, and the instructor will know to continue those behaviors or activities that you like.

About those picky rules: Yes, you must adhere to them. Most professors include a classroom rules and policies section on their syllabus. We understand that every professor has his or her own set of rules and that you have to adjust your behavior to each professor's particular requirements. This takes flexibility on your part—another skill that the college experience is designed to instill in you. Why do we have these rules? Assume that they have evolved over time. Professors may differ in their classroom rules due to the nature of their subject matter (e.g., science lab instructors will have different rules than an English instructor). Some rules, however, are designed by experience. Each time they have a negative classroom behavior experience, they realize that they need to add it to the syllabus so that it does not recur. This is unfortunate because it becomes a list of problem behaviors that few students engage in, but that when they do, are so disruptive to fellow students they inhibit learning. These include consequences for cheating, tardiness, missed work/exams, and obstreperous behaviors. Professors will obviously have different experiences, and so their syllabi will have different rules. The last thing you want to do is annoy the professor, so, take the classroom rules section of your course syllabi seriously, and learn what is expected in each class.

Do Student Course Evaluations Really Matter?

The academic job market is extremely competitive, with job ads listing numerous specialized qualifications. Sometimes hundreds of PhDs apply for one of what may be only two or three similar positions in the whole country. Even if you think your professor is incompetent or if you dislike him or her due to his or her quirks, understand that the person has made a rigorous cut. Professors all possess advanced training in their disciplines that can mean seven, eight, nine, or even more years of graduate school after college. You are expected to treat your professor with respect, even if he or she mumbles, has a foreign accent, stares at the wall when lecturing, wears funny clothes, or yes— even if he or she smells funny. They come from all over the world, and they bring their cultural traditions with them. That does not mean that you cannot help your professors adapt to their adopted culture or to the expectations of your generation. Expressing your concerns on the end-of-term student course evaluation will help. Following is a discussion of student evaluations in general and tips on how to write something that will truly help your professor improve the next time around.

Most schools have some form of student evaluation system in place. Student input is solicited on all aspects of a course, from the level of a professor's organization to the value of the course materials. We have heard that students do not take the student evaluations seriously because they do not think professors read them. Contrary to this belief, they do read them and they do take them seriously. Their evaluations are also read by the chairpersons of their departments and sometimes by the dean of the school. Professors and administrators who may review the evaluations generally dismiss comments that are out of line with what other students say. Comments that are harsh or rude generally get tossed out, because they are viewed as having been written by angry students who did not get good grades or who were troublemakers of some kind. Professors read evaluations with an eye toward comments that provide concrete suggestions for making the class run more smoothly or for deciding what material or aspects of the course to keep as is. Administrators read evaluations with an eye toward spotting any negative trends. Overall, if you want your concern (or even your praise) to be taken seriously, state it clearly, concisely, and professionally. Curtail emotional comments and offer specific suggestions for change. And of course, check your spelling and grammar so that you come across as a sophisticated communicator and as someone to whom your professors will want to listen.

▷ *Examples of Comments That Will Be Taken Seriously*

- ► "If you make changes to the syllabus, please post them online so that we will have an updated copy to use."

- ► "The second exam covered too much material that we did not discuss in class. I was taken by surprise, because we *did* discuss everything that was on the first exam."

- ► "I loved all of the field trips! Keep them!"

- ► "I didn't like the textbook. It had a lot of typos and inconsistent information. Some of the information in the textbook was different from the information given in class. This was confusing."

- ► "The work you gave us to do was very difficult, but my friend in someone else's math class clearly isn't learning as much as I am."

▷ *Examples of Comments That Will Be Dismissed*

- ► "The teacher is a freak. Replace him!!"

- ► "This class SUCKED. Why do we have to take English classes anyway when my major is ECONOMICS?"

- ► "This class is too early."

- ► "He wears too much black."

- ► "The professor Grades to hard on writting!" (Yes, one of us really did receive this comment!)

- ► "That D I earned in your class didn't help my grade point average, but it helped me get an A in my other statistics class."

What If I Have Problems with a Class or Instructor?

If your class performance concerns you, always talk with the professor first and then talk with your advisor about your options. If you have a specific issue regarding the professor (e.g., inappropriate behavior), talk with your advisor, with a professor you trust, with the department chairperson, with a counselor (free counseling services are offered at most schools), or with the dean of students. If you think you are being harassed by a professor or a graduate student, or receiving unwanted attention or comments, you should absolutely contact one of the school's professionals mentioned. Do not assume that you can handle the situation on your own. Please do not worry about getting the individual in trouble. The latter is not your problem. It is important to report these instances so that you and other students can be protected.

Why Does My Roommate Get Up So Early?
GETTING ALONG WITH PEOPLE WHO ARE DIFFERENT FROM YOU

One of the biggest surprises, and most important life lessons learned in college, is that not everyone is like you. In fact, your school works hard to ensure that the campus is diverse so that you can refine your interpersonal skills. They do this by recruiting the best faculty members from all over the world and by admitting a student body from a wide range of cultures, religions, races, and socioeconomic backgrounds. They also focus on recruiting students who may be like you in many ways, but who bring a different viewpoint or mindset to campus. You may be one of many Hispanic Catholics at your school, for instance, but are you a Hispanic Catholic who is deaf, or who is passionate about feminist politics, or who survived childhood leukemia and wants to become a doctor? Knowing how to relate to many different kinds of people is one hallmark of a college-educated individual. On the micro level, this skill may help you in the workforce when you need to manage a diverse staff or travel with fellow employees. On the macro level, educating people to relate well to each other has implications for world peace. The better we understand each other, the more harmonious the world will be.

College classrooms will address the issue of diversity in both formal and informal ways. Formally, a professor's course might be specifically tailored to include some level of diversity. For example, a reading list might cover works by authors from across different cultures. Also within the context of diversity, a course might include various and conflicting viewpoints related to one specific topic (people do things because of their genes; no, because of their upbringing; no, because of a mix of the two). More subtly, your professors are hired because they are the best at what they do. Since most academic institutions are equal opportunity employers, their employees can come from almost anywhere and espouse almost any belief system. Even in the smallest, most rural of schools you might find an English professor from Sierra Leone or have a Swiss physics instructor. Being willing to learn from them, and maybe learning more about their cultures and experiences will enhance your college experience.

If you live on campus, interacting with roommates and others in a dormitory situation will also further your diversity education. In this instance, the diversity lesson relates to learning how to coexist—in often close quarters—with people whose basic living styles differ from yours. In regards to roommates and dorm-mates, expect the unexpected. Although they often become lifelong friends, you might also find it difficult to connect with them. For instance, you will learn that some people might not be as polite or forgiving as you expect them to be. You might have roommates who borrow your things, who play their music while you are trying to sleep, who do not know or want to know how to clean, who are too clean, who have guests sleep over without your permission, or who do not like you or something about you. You may find yourself surprised to find that the students who live in the rooms around you practice religious rituals with which you are unfamiliar and that you find unsettling. Some people you will be able to live with easily, others you will not. The experience promises to be eye-opening in all cases.

How do you handle these differences? The first step is being cautious and simply understanding that people come with all sorts of expectations—and sometimes hang-ups. Sit down with your new roommate and discuss both of your expectations. Do you expect lights out at 11:00 P.M., or do you expect to be able to stumble back to your dorm room at 3:00 A.M.? Discuss this openly. Hopefully, you will match. If you encounter problems, however, see what you can do to work them out. A good way to think about your relationship with your roommate is to view it as a laboratory for learning how to handle interpersonal problems after graduation.

In fact, roommate difficulties can teach you as much about managing conflict as about diversity. If you resolve roommate issues successfully—which may include simply learning how to tough out a less-than-ideal situation—you will feel more confident in managing these types of relationships in the future (think about working with a demanding coworker or boss). Since you live with your roommate, you might even acquire some skills that will eventually help you negotiate living with a spouse. Do understand that you are not expected to handle every problem yourself. Some students enter college with preexisting or undiagnosed psychological disorders, and this is not something you should manage. Likewise, you should not have to live with someone

Image courtesy of Miami Dade College - North Campus

who engages in illegal activities or activities that interfere with your studies. Seek help if needed. Your dorm coordinator or **resident advisor** (a student employed to manage dorm occupants), academic advisor, and the university counseling center are useful resources, just as your company's human resources office will be there for you when you experience coworker problems.

We outlined some of the basic issues because they are a large part of your college experience. In high school, your parents may have handled household issues and helped smooth over conflicts between you and your siblings. In college, resolving these conflicts is your responsibility. You might lose sleep due to the decisions you make or that others around you make. Despite living issues that arise, you must still make it to class and do the work. This is part of the expectation that you are an adult, and it is good practice for life after graduation.

Did He Really Say That?!
PRACTICING CIVILITY

The theme of civility is a hot topic on college campuses. It is related, in part, to diversity. As a member of a college community, you are expected to take the time to understand those who are different from you and to treat them with respect—or in a civil manner. This means listening closely to people who might have different political views from you, possibly engaging in a heated debate, but ultimately agreeing to disagree rather than engaging in name-calling or completely disengaging. It means learning to identify sexist language, racial slurs, and demeaning adjectives and eliminating them from your vocabulary. It means refraining from making negative comments about anyone. It means taking time to reflect on why some beliefs and practices make you very uncomfortable. While the underlying theme of civility is tolerance, civility does not mean accepting people who are close minded, mean-spirited, or—worst-case scenario—violent. This kind of behavior is not productive to society. Ultimately, you will learn that there are some people with whom you cannot be friends, but with whom you must still practice civility. Furthermore, you should be aware that extreme acts of incivility could lead to expulsion.

On a more general level, civility is another term for employing basic manners. With the advent of new technologies, such as social networking and text messaging, we may communicate with large groups of people instantly without interacting with them in person. It is much easier to say hurtful things online that we would not normally say in someone's presence. This is cowardly, especially when said anonymously. It is also easy to represent ourselves falsely, which may contribute to an underlying sense of distrust. (This would include, for instance, posing as someone else online and saying something untrue about yourself.) We spend so much time using new technologies that we are constantly pressed for time and stressed. The result of all of this is that people are less civil to each other, and manners often fall by the wayside.

To put it bluntly, your professors expect you to have good manners, to be kind, and to be honest. Practice good manners consistently during college, and you will be a role model for others who have not been lucky enough to take part in conversations about civility on a college campus. To begin, treat your instructors and your peers with respect, and you will receive the same in return. Leave bad attitudes; negativity; demanding, pushy or blaming behavior; and general rudeness at home. If you currently tend toward these habits, now is the time to reinvent yourself. People who project a positive attitude are much more likely to lead satisfying lives and to be successful at both work and home. Get help from the college counseling center if you feel overwhelmed. There are many resources to support you as you make a personal change.

You will also have to learn to identify incivility and how to handle it. In the classroom, your instructor will introduce you to appropriate behaviors for interaction and act as a role model and a moderator. But your behavior outside of the classroom will give you a true sense of your personal integrity. The truly civil person not only practices civility, but also does not tolerate the incivility of others. Reflect on the type of person you want to be. You hear several friends cruelly teasing someone—will you step in or find someone who will? You witness a group of individuals engaged in property damage— are you willing to notify campus security or find someone who is? How you act in very real situations like these is the true mark of your character.

Now that we have covered the basics on your role as a student, it is time to begin thinking about navigating your way toward graduation and a bachelor's degree. Choosing your classes with a plan of action in mind is just the beginning.

Glossary

APA style—American Psychological Association—dictated writing and citation style and format used by those in the social sciences.

CEO—chief executive officer, the highest managerial position in a company.

MLA style—Modern Languages Association–dictated writing and citation style and format used by those in the humanities.

Resident advisor—often an undergraduate student employed by student housing to manage dorm occupants. Also known as a dorm coordinator.

Résumé—a self-prepared document summarizing one's work experience, usually requested by employers.

Can I Really Expect to Graduate in Four Years?

4

Increasingly students are spending more than four years in college. Some take five, six, or even seven years to complete their degrees. Taking so long to complete an undergraduate program delays your entry into the workforce, delays your matriculation (enrollment) into graduate programs, and is costly. Late graduation causes students to accrue an enormous amount of **student loan** (money borrowed by a student) debt. Starting off life with a high debt-to-income ratio is financially crippling on a new graduate's salary. We are here to tell you that it is entirely possible to graduate in four years. In fact, colleges and universities structure their curricula to be completed in four years. Mainly returning and older students, who may have families, jobs, military commitments, and other responsibilities, and who attend school part time, may take longer to complete their degrees. If you are in the enviable position of starting college right after graduating from high school, make the most of your position and commit to graduating in four years. It simply involves repeatedly making good decisions.

This chapter contains information on resources available to you and on important procedures, such as the registration process, that will help you navigate your degree and keep you on a four-year track. We also cover common mistakes that are guaranteed to delay your graduation and teach you how to make sensible decisions regarding work and extra curricular activities—two areas that can affect your progress.

Professor Jamie Anzalotta, M.S.W

Image courtesy of Miami Dade College - North Campus

From Session 4 of *College Orientation*, First Edition. Karen Bendersky, Catherine M. Chastain-Elliott.

What Do You Mean I'm Not Graduating?!
RESOURCES THAT WILL HELP YOU STAY ON TRACK

Learn what resources are available for you and where to find them at your college or university. Check the college or university website for a description of resources or speak with someone at your campus advising center. Following are valuable resources that are common to most four-year schools.

How Do I Choose a Major?

The fastest route to degree completion is by choosing your major early and sticking to it. We know this is easier said than done, and for good reason. Many college students find it difficult to choose a life path before they know what paths are actually available. Even students who seem dedicated to completing a degree in a specific field of study (e.g., law) might change career paths when they reach middle adulthood. For others, their focus changes much earlier (we know someone who majored in music but went to graduate school in math). This is not unusual. We understand both the reluctance in making the commitment to one area of study and the inability to identify a major, but do not let this decision paralyze you. There is not necessarily a perfect correspondence between your major and where you go after graduation. Nonetheless, choosing your major is a very important first step to a successful college experience. The earlier it is done, the more focused you are, and the faster you graduate—which will save you time and money. Following are recommendations that will help you get started in deciding which major is for you.

Visit the college career center. Individuals at the career center can give you questionnaires designed to assess your interests and career suitability. Even if these assessments do not capture the "true you," it is worth the visit. Other materials are available here such as listings of corporations, listings of jobs and internships, and a staff dedicated to all issues related to determining a career and jobs within that career. Look through the opportunity postings for ideas on what types of careers exist. Most of us are familiar with the standard array of jobs (medicine and science, government, education, law, sales), but what about those important careers that are less known? How about becoming an urban planner, running an organic farm, or designing golf courses? What you will probably find is that a career is something you work into, rather than jump right into. Exceptions exist with nursing, medicine, and education, of course, but for most, the typical path will involve gaining important college skills and then bringing those skills to the entry level of some industry where you will work yourself into a career. Maybe you will start as a logistics coordinator for a wine company and eventually be promoted to vice president of wine logistics. Use this opportunity to see the breadth of career choices that exist.

Peruse your university's course catalog listings. Pay less attention to the department teaching the course than to the course description. Place a check mark next to all of the courses that look even remotely interesting to you. Next, identify trends:

1. Do most of the courses fall in a particular college/school (arts & sciences, business, law, education, or health sciences)?

2. Within that college/school, what area has the most check marks (math, sciences, arts, humanities, business administration, or technology)? and

3. What major has the most check marks?

The reason we recommend this strategy is that it allows you to see the bigger picture. If you immediately narrow your check marks down to a specific major, you could miss a side interest or another major that might actually better capture want you want. Seeing the bigger category also gives you a general sense of your focus, should you consider changing later. What if you find that one single major does not capture your interests? In such a case, consider taking on a minor or a second major. We recommend speaking with an academic advisor if you add a second major (also called *a double major*) or minor because completing your degree in four years will require careful tracking.

Work toward identifying your strong and weak points. We all have them. While we are not advocates of taking the easy route, we also do not want you to fool yourself. If, despite your best efforts, you have never been able to earn higher than a C in high school chemistry, then seriously reconsider pursuing a pre-med degree. Be realistic about your abilities. Try to make this self-assessment in the absence of family pressure to follow a particular path. You might find greater wisdom in the honest feedback of close friends. Additionally, do not be lured into believing that your strength should dictate your major. It does not have to. Your strength will remain with you no matter what you choose to do, and you will most likely apply it to whatever field you choose. Someone we know is a skilled fine arts painter but majored in a science. Interestingly, this person utilizes creative-thinking skills when designing unique scientific studies. Also, do not mistake fear for lack of ability. For example, we know someone who always had a tremendous fear of public speaking. She would never raise her hand in class, would shy away from classes that required presentations, and refused to take a rhetoric course. Obviously, this person never considered a major or career requiring public speaking. Oddly enough, after graduation this person was forced to teach a small class as part of her job duties. Though terrified in the beginning, she learned she had a tremendous capacity for teaching and found herself years later teaching to a class of over 400 students and enjoying it. Sometimes, our fears can mask our true strong points.

Make use of core (general education) classes and the opportunity presented by them to help you search for a major. Consider choosing courses that count toward your general education requirements but that might be a little outside of your interests. Likewise, if a class you want is closed, view this as an opportunity. Choose another class that counts toward the same requirement, but that pushes your boundaries. You might be surprised to find that you absolutely love a class that you would not have thought suited you. Most of us think we know what a course will be like, but we probably do not. Maybe the thought of taking an early-twentieth-century German literature course sounds awful, but you might be missing a special experience! Sometimes, the professor, rather than the topic, determines a lot of our interest in a subject. We know plenty of people who were steered away from a specific major because a single course with a specific professor turned them off. These same people report owing their enthusiasm toward an unexpected major to a professor who was passionate about the subject matter. Be willing to try something unexpected. Yes, there is the chance that you might hate the class and regret your decision. But you have still made progress toward your degree and gained the knowledge that the subject matter really is not for you.

Talk to college graduates about what they majored in and how it relates to their current career. Asking someone why they chose their major or career is a great ice breaker, and it will give you a good sense of what careers are out there and how to get into that career. You might find yourself at a family party standing next to the wife of your dad's business partner. You could just look awkwardly at each other, but why not ask her what she does, why she chose that path, and what she thinks about it. You might get some fantastic advice and potentially gain a valuable contact for the future.

Think long and hard about the lifestyle you might want—not just immediately after you graduate, but in ten or twenty years. Students sometimes spend so much time thinking about what career they want, that they do not consider *how* they want to live. If you think that salary is your number one priority, then you have it easy. You can do a web search and find the top paying careers. But, do you want the time commitment and lack of freedom that might come with that type of salary? For instance, you could become a quantitative analyst for an investment bank. You would make big money and live in a big, exciting city. You might also be expected to work 80 hours a week (including some weekends) and asked to sign a **nondisclosure agreement** (a legal document stipulating what information you can share with others and what you may do in your spare time). If that sounds good to you, then your choice is made. But if you were hoping to spend more time with your family or enjoy your hobbies, then maybe you need to shift your priorities. Likewise, how much time do you want to spend commuting? Do you want to travel a lot, only some, or not at all? Do you expect your own office, a cubicle environment, or a table that you share with others? What is your vision of the typical workweek? What time do you want to arrive at work and leave? What do you want to be able to wear? Will your work life allow you to raise children? You get the picture. Look around you and watch people working and living. Think deeply about your everyday expectations. When you have a good sense of what you hope to have, bring your ideas to the career center's staff and to your academic advisor. Your expectations will help guide their advice.

What Is the Role of an Academic Advisor?

Perhaps the most important resource for you while you are in college is your academic advisor. Depending on the school, you will either be automatically assigned to an academic advisor in your major, or you may request a specific faculty member. Get to know this person. He or she will help you choose your courses, direct you to appropriate resources, help you develop a career path, and help you apply for internships, jobs, and graduate school. Advisors can also tell you what is going on in the department and/or university and tell you about special opportunities (like a research opening with one of the other professors). If you want to change advisors, talk with the department secretary or the school's advising office. Remember, however, that professors serving as advisors are not expected to know everything in the university catalog or memorize all of the requirements for graduation. This is *your* responsibility, and the information is in the school catalog. Professors are better at advising you regarding their specific field of interest than about the school's specific and ever-changing degree requirements— although most of us do know a good deal about degree requirements in our particular discipline or major.

Please remember that it is your responsibility to put a schedule together for the upcoming term. You know best what times of day you would like your classes to start, how much time in between classes you need, and what conflicts you need to work around (like your sports team practice schedule). If you arrive for an advising appointment without a possible schedule, you will be asked to come back when you are prepared. Advising appointments are for general guidance (e.g., what classes are being offered that will help you meet a particular career goal as well as count toward your degree). Advising sessions are not for nuts-and-bolts questions like what section of a course you should take. That is up to you. Figuring out how to schedule your day by considering your options and making do with courses that are open and available is one way you learn independence in college. Since independence is one of those important skills that college is designed to equip you with, work on this skill during registration.

Unfortunately, you might encounter some professors who really do not want to advise you at all (possibly because they are pressed for time or do not feel like competent advisors), but they are required to do so as part of their workload. This kind of advisor might simply do a cursory glance over your schedule and then give his or her okay. He or she will assume you have done your homework and know what you need to take. This is a good reason to stay on top of your progress and read the course catalog.

One last bit of information about academic advisors is that they are not counselors. Advisors are a great first stop if you are having a problem in virtually any area of your life, but ultimately, they are not qualified mental health counselors. They absolutely care about you, and so they will point you to the right person or office if you are experiencing personal difficulties or send you to the correct resource if you have academic issues and need tutorial support. If you are a younger student (i.e., 18–21) and are close to your parents, you might want to share with them that advisors are not counselors. In recent years, parents have become increasingly involved in their students' lives at college—to the point that they call or email professors and share very personal information about you (e.g., "Sally suffers from anxiety and is having difficulty concentrating in class due to a new medication").

How Do I Use the Undergraduate Course Catalog?

Read your college or university's course catalog. There is usually a copy available online. Your college catalog should be considered your college bible. All freshmen are admitted under a particular catalog and its specific curriculum (the courses offered and those needed to obtain your degree). It is important to remember your particular catalog year, because the curriculum continually changes. The catalog is updated every year, but you usually need to fulfill only the requirements that were outlined in *your* freshman catalog. To be sure that you know your specific course requirements, download or print relevant sections of your catalog (both the general education requirements and your major requirements). Do not lose these copies. Should there be a disagreement at graduation time, you may need the copies to prove that you have fulfilled all of the university's requirements for graduation. Be aware that some schools allow you to change catalogs under specific circumstances. If you think that changing your catalog would benefit you, be sure that the school officially approves this change. Also, please weigh the possibility that changing your catalog midstream will likely cause you to lose some course credits, and you will be required to take additional courses. Consult your academic advisor or the **registrar's office** (the unit that maintains student records and manages student registration) whenever you have questions.

In addition to curriculum information, the catalog includes a summary of each course offered at your university. If you want to know what ANTH 210 is, for instance, the catalog will tell you it is a mid-level anthropology class. It also contains information such as how to obtain a minor, what kinds of student services are available, what types of financial aid are available, and facts about registration. In short, the course catalog can answer almost any question you have about your college or at least point you to the right person for further help. If you understand the catalog, you can almost graduate without ever consulting with an advisor (it is that thorough!). Sometimes, your faculty advisor may not be able to answer all of your advising questions and may inadvertently answer some of your questions incorrectly. Remember, the catalog can *change year to year,* and though we earnestly strive to advise you correctly, sometimes professors are not aware of every single change that has been made.

To say it once more, always consult the catalog—the one for *your* entering year. Most contain a disclaimer that the information in the catalog, and not an advisor's advice, is the official word on degree requirements. Getting bad advice from an advisor may hold up your graduation date for any number of reasons. Your advisor may ultimately be reprimanded for advising you poorly (if you can prove that he or she did indeed give you false information), but your college will not step in and waive requirements for you so that you can graduate on time. In college, *you* are entirely responsible for when and if you graduate.

How to Decode the Course Numbering System

- Each university has its own abbreviation and numbering system (e.g., BIO 210, ENGL 1101).

- Freshmen courses have the lowest numbers (e.g., 100 or 1100) with the designated numbers increasing by year. The highest numbers are for graduate-level courses.

- This system helps you determine whether the course is at the appropriate level for you. Freshmen, in general, should not take a 300- or 3000-level course, even if the computer registration system allows you to sign up for one.

- Professors tailor their courses according to this numbering system. Lower-numbered courses are usually survey courses in which the professor does not expect the student to have prior knowledge of the subject matter. At the higher levels, a course might have a prerequisite (a course you must take before you can sign up for the upper-level course), or the professor might expect a certain level of background knowledge, work, and decorum from the student.

What Is on the College Website?

Most colleges have a very thorough and well-organized website for undergraduates. Bookmark it and *use* it. Ideally, you did this before arriving on campus. There will be web pages devoted specifically to student success, student life, sports, art events, and campus speakers. Usually, the registration portal will be on your school's website. You will probably be able to reserve a room for a club meeting online, sign up for an appointment in the student health center, or help a friend to the counseling center. At the end of each term, you will be able to find out your course grades by going online.

What Department Resources Are Available?

Individual academic departments will have several resources to help you maneuver through your major. The person who knows the most about the department is the department chairperson. The administrative assistant will also be knowledgeable, and this person is often more accessible than the chairperson. However, the administrative assistant's job is not to serve every student's needs. This person mainly helps out the faculty with their day-to-day tasks. But do not be afraid to stop in at a department's front office and ask for help. Other resources include a department website, which is designed to assist students in the major. It might list a four-year sample plan for your major and the complete list of degree requirements.

It will also list the department's entire faculty, their contact information and office locations, their specific areas of expertise, and where they earned their degrees. The departmental website might also list links to lab websites or to resources such as the music library or art gallery. Sometimes, the website will even include testimonials from current students or recent graduates about their accomplishments and professional plans.

What Is the Registrar's Office?

The registrar's office keeps an official record of each student's progress toward his or her degree. If you have any questions about degree or graduation requirements, the registrar can answer them. This office manages the registration process and usually oversees special requests. These requests may include overseeing waitlists for courses, managing the approval process for students who have been allowed to overload into a class (or add the class even though it is full), organizing requests from students who want to take more than the allowed number of credit hours, and removing holds placed on students' accounts that are keeping them from registering. The registrar also handles transfer issues such as what courses transfer in from another school and what courses might transfer out. At the end of your college experience, the registrar's office is where you will request your official transcript.

Is Tutoring Available?

Colleges and universities offer a variety of help for students who are struggling academically or who want to get ahead. Sometimes, a school has one tutoring center, that oversees all forms of academic help, and sometimes it may have specific offices for specific issues. Extra help with language classes, for instance, may occur in the language lab. An academic success or an academic excellence office may provide academic help for students on **academic probation** (the status of those with a GPA so low, they are in danger of being dismissed from the college) or who are working through a remedial course of study.

How Can the Writing Center Help Me?

Most colleges have writing centers. The purpose of a writing center is to help you improve your writing skills. Excellent—not merely acceptable—writing skills are a hallmark of the college-educated individual. Those who write extremely well, using the rules of standard edited English, get ahead. In college, your professors expect you to apply all of the grammar rules and organizational skills you learned in high school and to build on your basic abilities. There is truth in the saying, "Writing is 10% inspiration and 90% perspiration." It takes hard work, and all writing can be improved. Good writing involves critiquing and editing. The writing center will help you identify any personal or recurring writing issues and help you with individual writing assignments. In general, be aware that writing center tutors do not proofread. Tutors also cannot tell you if the content of your writing is correct (they might not have knowledge of your specific subject matter), but they can tell you whether you are communicating the information effectively and using style guidelines and formats appropriately.

What Is the Speech Center?

Another important skill to develop during college is the ability to confidently convey information orally. This is why many schools now provide speech centers. The purpose of the speech center is to help you prepare for oral presentations. You might receive feedback on your presentation skills or get help putting together specific speeches or presentations. Sometimes, you will be videotaped so you can see how you come across to an audience. The speech center might also help you correct any strong grammar or dialect problems. Most people find public speaking absolutely intimidating, but in your future you will likely have to engage in it. Taking advantage of this resource now will help you develop skills to impress your future boss or even your best friend, when you offer a toast at his or her wedding.

What Is the Language Lab?

Language labs help you learn to speak a foreign language. You may learn how to read in a foreign language in the classroom, and you may also speak that language in the classroom. In order to truly master a language, however, you must practice speaking it out loud. The language lab has resources to help you learn to effectively listen and communicate in nonnative languages. This is another resource that deserves your attention during college. After college, you will have to pay good money for a lesser resource and experience. Did you know that bilingual speakers get higher salaries in a number of fields?

What Do I Need to Know about Computer Centers and Technology Support?

Most campuses offer a variety of technology support. There are computer labs, usually staffed with knowledgeable workers, where you may use computers and print work. Many campuses have a help desk where you can go or call to ask specific questions about software or to get help with courses or assignments requiring technology. Often, you are able to get free programs for, or servicing of, your personal computer. You may also be able to check out certain kinds of computer equipment from a computer lab, the library, or another area. Sometimes, technology resources are associated with specific academic areas (for instance, a music technology lab may be located in the music department), and sometimes they are located in a central area. Familiarize yourself with your institution's technology resources and make use of them. After all, your fees help pay for these services and equipment.

Image courtesy of Miami Dade College - North Campus

How Can the International Students and/or Study Abroad Office Help Me?

Students who are not U.S. citizens need help transitioning to the American college system, and to the local culture, when they enroll. If you fall into this category, your school's version of an international students or programs office will help you find your way through the system. The office will educate you about rules and policies that may affect you, such as how many credit hours you need to maintain in order to keep your student visa (if you are required to have one; students from certain countries do not need visas.) This office may also oversee study abroad programs for students wishing to spend a term or a year taking classes in another country. Studying abroad is an eye-opening experience, but one that must be planned well in advance. Be sure to talk to a study abroad advisor about your plans early so you can identify what classes will transfer back to your home institution. This office will also provide you with guidance on filling out all required paperwork and will give you practical information, such as what vaccinations you might need to get in order to remain healthy in another country.

What Is the Role of Student Disability Services?

Disability offices offer specialized support and individualized education for people who come to college and who have a disability. The first step is for students to make an appointment at the office, preferably right before the start of their first term, in order to provide official documentation of their disability. This can be a physical disability or a learning disability. If you do not document your disability, the university is not legally allowed to offer you special consideration. If you do, you will be given what you need, within reason, to perform better in your courses. Some students are embarrassed to document their disabilities, and they do not receive the help they need. Be proactive and get help before you run into trouble. Remember that you do not need to make use of special considerations just because you have the documentation. Get your documentation taken care of at the outset, and then you are free to use it when and if you think you need to.

What Can the Career Center Do for Me?

All students should visit their college's career services center early in their freshman year, and at least once during their sophomore and junior year to see what careers are in demand as they approach graduation. Early on, the career center will help you target careers that fit your personality, your working style, and other preferences. They can tell you about jobs that you may not even know existed, or that you knew about but thought would not be a good fit for you. This knowledge may help you determine your major or minor. Later in your college career, stop by for help with writing your résumé and learning how to interview. The career center will also post information on career fairs and on-campus corporate recruitment for seniors and new graduates. If you actively seek help in the career center, you are much more likely to get a good job when you graduate or have a job waiting for you upon graduation.

What Is the Bursar's Office?

In order to use any of the previously outlined resources, you must pay your tuition, room, and board bills. The bursar's office is where you pay bills. If you do not pay your bills by a certain date, a hold may be placed on your registration, or your registration may be cancelled. If your registration is cancelled, you will loose your classes and someone else may take your spot. Once you lose your spot and a class is full, you will be stuck creating an entirely new schedule. Your professors may even be told that you are not allowed to attend classes. Please plan well in advance to have your bills paid on time, or pay them on time yourself, so you can continue to use campus support services (tutoring center, career center, the technology support center, and library). When in doubt, contact this office to check on your payment status.

What Can I Expect from the Financial Aid Office?

Most students cannot afford to pay the full amount of their college tuition, room, board, and other bills in total. The financial aid office puts together a package of financial tools to help make college affordable for you. This is known as a **financial aid package** and may include a mixture of scholarships (free money for exceptional students), loans (money that you will have to pay back when you graduate); grants (free money based on you or your family's unique financial situation), work-study opportunities (money that you will work for on campus), and a reduced amount of tuition money that you will have to pay up front. Usually, your financial aid package is put together for you before you even arrive on campus. Stop by your college's financial aid office at any point if you or your family's financial situation changes. And remember, sometimes parts of your aid, especially scholarships, depend on you maintaining a certain GPA or carrying out certain duties. Make sure that you are aware of what you must do in order to keep your financial aid.

Table 1 Financial Aid Options

Type of Funding	Description
Scholarship	Awarded based on merit; may have to keep a certain GPA or fulfill other duties in order to keep it; does not have to be paid back; usually runs out after four years.
Loan	Money borrowed from a bank or other source that you must begin paying back, plus interest, soon after graduation; payments are monthly, last many years, and increase with the amount you borrow.
Grant	Awarded based on a student's financial situation; reserved for those who have few financial resources; does not have to be paid back; usually runs out after four years.
Work study	Money earned from a campus job specifically created to help with school and living expenses; does not have to be paid back.
Tuition reduction	Reduced tuition offered for a certain number of years to those with a financial need; does not have to be paid back.

Do I Really Have to Take an 8:00 A.M. Class?
DEALING WITH REGISTRATION REALITIES

Registration is an important part of every term. Begin working on your options a couple of weeks before your registration time slot opens, because it is not always easy to figure out what you need to take and when to take it. Create an ideal schedule with classes you need and times you need to take them and several alternate schedules. Base this schedule on reality: check the days and times the courses are offered (if they are offered at all; not all courses are offered every term). Watch to make sure classes you want do not close. Plan a full course load each term. Finally, be prepared to work through some of the following issues, and do not be afraid to seek advice from your academic advisor. Just be prepared, with specific questions, when you make an appointment to speak to him or her.

Will There Really Be Closed Classes?

Classes will fill up quickly or simply will not be offered. This is common to all universities. You will need to consider taking classes that you had not previously planned on. There is nothing wrong with this as long as you take classes that still fulfill graduation requirements. You may discover new areas of study and expand your interests, stumble upon a great professor who changes your life, or even discover your major. If you really need a class, consider asking the professor if he or she can possibly add another student. Be aware that most professors do not have the time, the classroom space, or sometimes the equipment needed to teach an additional student; classes are capped at a certain number of students for many reasons. We recommend that you keep checking your school's online registration site to determine when/if a seat opens during the drop/add period. Students do a lot of course dropping and adding during the first week of classes, and you may get a seat. Also consider taking a summer class to help keep you on pace with graduating in four years.

Will I Have to Take Classes on Fridays and Early Mornings?

That's right, some classes are offered only on a Monday/Wednesday/Friday schedule. There is no sound reason to skip classes on Fridays. If you do not want to take Friday classes, ask yourself if you are truly committed to obtaining a college degree. Some universities hold classes on Saturdays, too, and as early as 6:30 A.M. Especially as a freshman, you will need to take the courses you can get and make do. This might mean no three-day weekends to visit your boyfriend's or girlfriend's school, or to go home to do laundry, or to hang out at the beach. It might also mean that you have to take the worst work hours at your part-time job. Just remember that your hard work will pay off, and you will graduate in four years, owing much less money. Plus, you will hone your ability to consistently work toward long-term goals—yet another valuable life skill—instead of giving in to immediate gratification. Realize that as you acquire more credits, your registration time slot moves up and you will begin to get your pick of the best classes and time slots.

What Are Registration Holds?

Holds prevent you from registering, and you must resolve them at the business office, registrar's office, or other office on campus. The reasons for a hold might include unpaid tuition, an outstanding parking ticket, library fines, or financial aid issues. At some schools, your academic advisor may put a hold on your registration until you meet with him or her to approve your class schedule. Check to make sure there are no holds on your registration account several days before you register, so that you will have time to resolve them.

What Are Prerequisites?

The course for which you are registering might require a **prerequisite** (a lower-level course that acts as a stepping-stone into the desired course). Make sure that you have taken the necessary prerequisite courses before you attempt to register. If you are currently taking the prerequisite course but the computer system will not acknowledge it, contact your advisor or the registrar's office so that you can fix the problem immediately.

What Do I Need to Know about Labs?

Many courses (sciences, languages, others) require a lab. If they do, you will have to take the lab at the same time as the main course. If you are retaking a science course you previously failed but happened to pass the lab, you probably do not need to retake the lab. Contact the appropriate department to learn more.

What's Wrong with Dropping a Class?
AIMING FOR ON-TIME GRADUATION

As academic advisors, we often see students make mistakes that have a negative impact on their academic careers. We warn of these actions, and sometimes even refuse to sign forms giving our permission if we think a student is taking counter-productive steps. Unfortunately, at most schools, the lack of an advisor's signature on paperwork is not enough to halt what we know is a risky decision: even without our signature, for instance, you may still be able to drop a class. You hold ultimate control over earning your degree on time. This section outlines several common actions that may cause you to get off course.

Why Is It Important to Graduate in Four Years?

There are many reasons why you should strive to complete your degree in four years. Several relate to finances. First, most scholarships run out after four years. This means that if you are not finished with your degree in four years, you or your family may be in for a shock when you see the rise in your tuition bill for each additional term needed to graduate. Second, if you are funding your education through loans, each additional term will increase the cost of your monthly payoff bill once you graduate. It is a good idea to contact your lender(s) once a year and ask how much your monthly bill would be if you were to leave school at that point. This will serve as a reality check and may motivate you to finish sooner. A good way to get a grasp on how loan payments will affect the quality of your life after you graduate is to think in terms of car payments. If you owe $300 per month in loan payments, this is the equivalent of an average car payment. If you get a typical entry-level job, this may mean that you do not get a new car (or any car) when you graduate. Third, you may want a graduate degree, and you may need to borrow money to keep yourself (and possibly, if you are older, your spouse and family) afloat during this process. These additional loans will compound what you owe on a monthly basis.

Nonfinancial reasons exist for graduating within four years. A major one is that your friends and support group start graduating without you, and you begin to feel detached from the college or university without them. This makes graduating even more difficult. Moreover, if you go to a university where most students are of a traditional age (18 to 22), you eventually become older than most students, which may make you feel out of place. Finally, your transcript will reveal an extended college career and will suggest to employers that you have difficulty focusing and completing long-range goals.

Our experience has shown there are several common actions or decisions that extend student academic careers. As you read through the following points, remember that doing one of these things, even once, can add an entire term to your college career, even if that means staying around to complete just one more class. Imagine what taking several of these detrimental actions can do to hold up your graduation. Do not let this be you! It is never too late to get back on track—the sooner the better.

What Are Common Mistakes That Will Delay My Graduation?

Mistake 1: *Experimenting to find the right major by taking lots of classes that do not give you credit toward your degree.* We call this procrastination. Each individual could potentially do well in any number of majors; you simply need to look seriously at your options, chose a major, and then stick to your decision. Make a pact with yourself to keep going in your chosen major, even during those difficult terms when one of your required classes turns out to be more difficult than you thought, outright boring, not your thing, or if a professor leaves you with a bad taste in your mouth for the field. All of this happens to everyone. The best students do not let these experiences influence them to the point that they change majors, as they know this will set them back.

A reminder of the best steps to take to choose a major: Skim the entire college course catalog—it does not take long—and narrow your list down to two or three majors based on your interests and personality. Take introductory-level classes in those areas *that also count toward your general education or core curriculum requirements.* If you experiment in this way, your classes will give you credit toward your degree, even if you decide not to major in the area associated with a course. For example, if you think you might want to major in chemistry, test the waters by taking one of the chemistry classes that count toward your general education requirements instead of one that simply looks interesting. If you still cannot make a decision after taking this approach, talk to as many professors and students as you can about the major and find out more about it. Also try stopping by the career center to take personality and aptitude tests that will point you in the direction of your strengths.

In general, avoid taking the advanced classes in a discipline unless you are sure that you want to major in it. Remember, you can always add on a minor in another academic field if you have time and then go into that area when you graduate. Sometimes, employers and graduate schools just want to see that you have taken the main classes in a discipline; a complete major is not necessary.

Mistake 2: *Thinking that you can take anything to fulfill your electives.* **Electives,** or classes that count toward neither your general education requirements nor your major, but that give you credit hours toward the overall number of hours needed for graduation, are often not really classes that you can take just for fun. They are generally used up in one of several situations.

Say you are required to take four electives. Theoretically, these can be anything. But what if your math SAT score is low and your school requires you to take a lower-level math class before allowing you to take one of the math classes that actually count toward your general education program? Where does the lower-level class count?

Some schools will allow you to count it as one of your required electives, but only if you have an elective class left. Otherwise, the lower-level class may get you behind and you may find yourself having to stay an extra term just to finish a *single* class. Or, say that you take AP (advanced placement) art history in high school, but find on arriving that your college does not give credit in the core curriculum fine arts area for AP art history. The school will most likely give you hours toward graduation for the class but require that you take another art class to satisfy the fine arts requirement. You might be able to plug this AP class into an electives slot instead but, again, only if you have an elective slot left. Similarly, if you change your major after already taking three or four advanced courses in a discipline, you may be able to stay on track, despite your indecision, if you still have electives slots open to put the courses in. Finally, you may want to eventually put additional classes not required for your major, but strongly suggested by your academic advisor, in your electives slots. Imagine getting to your senior year, seeing the wisdom in your advisor's suggestion to take a class, and not being able to take advantage of it (without an extra term in college) because you have already taken all of your electives. All of these situations are common, and there are many more such instances. So, think long and hard before you take a class just for fun—at least early in your college career.

Mistake 3: Transferring to a new school without a good reason. There is currently a national epidemic of students transferring between schools. Some transfer more than once. As a result, students are taking much longer to obtain their degrees and are racking up enormous amounts of student loan debt. The main reason why transferring can automatically put you on the five-year plan is that every college and university has a different core curriculum, or general education sequence, and different requirements and courses for majors. If you take music appreciation at college 1, for instance, to satisfy what may be called an aesthetics requirement, you may find yourself at college 2 facing a general education curriculum that a) does not include this class, and b) has no aesthetics requirement. The class will be a wasted credit (though not necessarily an intellectual waste) unless college 2 will give you elective credit for it, which may or may not be the case. Or say that you take biology for non majors at college 1. College 2 may require that majors and non majors, alike, take the same introductory biology class to keep the standards the same. You are thus forced to retake introductory biology or another science, even though you know most of the material. This is a waste of your time and tuition money. And what if you started a major in economics at college 1, only to find that the economics major at college 2 requires a slightly different set of classes? Each of these scenarios is common. So remember, transferring almost always puts you on the five-year plan—or longer.

Some students change schools to major in an area not offered at their first school. Before doing so, talk to a professor at your current school who is in a related discipline. Quite often, you can major in a related field, add a few classes on top of that, and achieve the exact same program of study as if you had transferred. For instance, a student who decides to become an art conservator, but does not have the choice to major in art conservation at her school, could obtain preparation for the career by majoring in chemistry and minoring in art history. Employers and graduate schools want to see only the classes; they often do not care what the major is called.

If you plan to transfer to another school despite this guidance—one with a stronger reputation, for instance—you must do well in the courses you are currently taking. Your top-choice school will not admit you if you do not show that you are capable of handling college-level work. Perhaps more importantly, you want to do well because most students who intend to transfer never do. Thus, your poor initial performance (and quite possibly your behavior) will remain on your record. Finally, it is important to remember that future employers or graduate schools will ask for transcripts from all the universities you attended (regardless of whether you obtained your degree from there). Thus, *all* of your grades (not to mention the number of times that you transfer) will be seen.

Mistake 4: *Leaving school to "find yourself."* If you find yourself unable to choose a major and are burned out on school in general, do your best to finish out the term with acceptable grades. Then spend the next term getting college credit, instead of no credit, doing an internship, which is an off-campus work experience in your area of interest. Choose an internship that allows you to continue exploring an area that interests you, even if you are kind of burned out on the whole "political science thing" (or pre law, nursing, criminal justice, or whatever your intended major is). Doing an internship in the area that interested you enough to consider majoring in it quite often resparks your interest and helps you realize that school, in general, is a lot of work, but a career in your chosen field, after completing your studies, will be much more exciting. (Plus, it will give you a paycheck!) If you are simply craving a change of scenery, try studying abroad for a term through one of your school's approved programs (note we said *approved*; preapprove all study-abroad classes to make sure they count toward your degree at your home school). Doing so will not only broaden your horizons, but you will come home refreshed and having completed courses toward your general education requirements or your major.

If you are too burned out to even do an internship or study abroad, our advice to you is this: Remember that summer is just around the corner, and you can rest and regroup then. Our best students almost always get burned out—they work extremely hard in their courses—but they are able to rest and refocus during the summer months. You can, too.

Mistake 5: *Missing your registration time slot due to being unprepared or unsure what to take.* While you are getting your act together, other people are taking the available slots in the classes that you could have signed up for had you been ready. The classes you want or need will close while you think about what you should take.

Mistake 6: *Not registering for classes that meet at times that you do not like.* Everyone, especially freshmen and sophomores, must take classes at inconvenient times, for

Professor Lottie M. Tucker-McMillan, M.Ed.

Image courtesy of Miami Dade College - North Campus

instance, at 8:00 A.M. We find that students will often substitute a fun class instead of taking an early morning class just to have a full load. The result: That is one more class you are going to have to take later, possibly even at—you guessed it— 8:00 A.M. Maybe that class is taught by a professor who always teaches it at 8:00 A.M. Be aware that not all classes are taught every term. What if that 8:00 A.M. class is taught only once a year or once every *two* years? And what if it is a prerequisite for another class, and you failed to take it when it was offered? You run the risk of putting yourself very far behind in situations such as these.

Similarly, some students avoid classes that meet on Fridays so that they can take frequent long weekend trips or go home (thus contributing to their college's reputation as a "suitcase school"). There is no sound reason to avoid taking classes on Fridays. If you do not want to take Friday classes then what exactly is your commitment to school? Some universities hold classes on Saturday, too. In general, we find that students who take minivacations during the middle of the term have one foot out the door. Not only does scheduling your classes this way cause problems of the kind just mentioned, but serious students know that they need to be on campus on the weekends to study. Resources like language labs, science/research labs, libraries, music repositories, and art studios are on campus, and you need them to get your assignments done. Time-wise, everyone knows that college is *more* than a full-time job. If you find that you have enough time for weekend trips, you are not giving college your full attention and may be headed for poor grades.

Mistake 7: If you commute, deciding that you will come to campus only on certain days. It will be difficult for you to complete your degree if you come to campus only on days that you prefer. Some courses are offered year after year on the same schedule, and at some point, you will need to make arrangements to be on campus to take them. Staying off campus on certain days is an especially easy way miss taking prerequisite classes, which are important lower-level courses that you *must* take before enrolling in advanced courses. No doubt, there will be many terms when it works out that you need to be on campus only Monday/Wednesday/Friday, or Tuesday/Thursday. But avoid deciding in advance that this is the way it is going to be. If you have an excuse for avoiding campus on certain days, make sure that it is a good one—for instance, you have kidney dialysis on Wednesdays and must be at the hospital to receive your treatment. (That being said, we find that our best students successfully work around even difficult situations such as this.) It is a good idea to line up your transportation *after* you know your class schedule, and to find a part-time job that allows you some flexibility in work hours so that you can be on campus when you need to.

Returning adult students who have families and full-time jobs to consider will no doubt find it more difficult than most to be on campus each day. Most of your professors will understand your position, but avoid asking for special considerations such as being allowed to come to class fifteen minutes late each period or to skip a certain day of each week entirely. If you have childcare issues (for instance, during the week of your child's spring break), and want to make an effort to be on campus anyway, please note that many professors will want to accommodate you and will graciously allow you to bring your child to class. But remember that even the most well-behaved children may distract your classmates when they whisper loudly that they are ready for a snack, or that they finished their coloring project, or that they need to go to the bathroom.

Mistake 8: Working off campus or working more than ten hours per week. If you are of traditional college age and are responsible for only your own immediate bills such as your cell phone, or **fraternity/sorority** dues (beyond tuition, room, and board, which you pay before the term begins), try to get a job on or adjacent to campus to save time and gas money. If you must work more than ten hours per week, as do many students for a variety of reasons, it is really best to go to school part time. Your ability to handle the demands of college and to get the most out of your tuition money, is greatly compromised if you register for a full load and then also work full time. We find that younger, less mature students who work more than ten hours per week often underperform, fall asleep in class, miss class, find themselves making excuses, and need extra help from instructors. These students miss important developmental and résumé-building opportunities by failing to participate in organizations, workshops, volunteer work, and experiential learning opportunities. They are quite often stressed, angry, and frustrated. Although students who go to school full time and also work full time may manage such a hectic schedule for a term or two, they eventually burn out. When you receive poor grades as a result of not having enough time to study outside of class, you will regret having made this mistake. If you need to work because you have made a poor decision (buying a new car, which comes with monthly payments) or running up credit cards on luxuries, you need to work on your finances.

Mistake 9: Withdrawing from classes. If you withdraw from a class—even one time in a major that requires many credit hours—you are probably putting yourself on a five-year plan. You also risk dropping below full-time status, which comes with its own set of issues. For instance, if you are a non-U.S. citizen, your student visa may be affected. You usually have one week at the start of each term to determine whether your course selection is going to be too much for you to handle. Be sure to check how much time you have to make schedule changes at your school. Read the syllabus for each course you are signed up for and skim over any assignment details posted online. Look at the textbooks and all required readings. Make a note of when all of your assignments for each of your classes will be due. Decide if you can realistically be successful with your class combination as it is or if you are setting yourself up for getting a D, or worse, in one of the classes. If you find that you are in over your head, change before the drop/add period ends, but be sure to pick up something else more suitable, but also required, so that you do not get behind by having too few credit hours.

If you withdraw from a class after the official drop/add period ends, the registrar at most schools will place a W on your transcript. Many students do not realize that future employers and graduate schools may interpret a W as your inability to get organized or to know what you can handle. They may also see you as someone who gives up when the going gets rough. Likewise, a faculty member who you want to use as a job or graduate school reference may review your transcript and report that you lack perseverance. In general, repeated indications of W on your transcript may signal work-habit issues on your part.

Mistake 10: Failing classes. You have wasted your time and money and must repeat the class. Some schools have a **grade forgiveness** policy, which means that you may repeat a certain number of courses—usually two or three—for a better grade. If your school has such a policy, forget that it exists. It may encourage you to think, "I will just retake this class for a better grade if I do not do well." If you believe this, you are almost guaranteed to fail. But what if you find out halfway through that you can manage the material, and the F you earned might actually have been a C if you had applied yourself the whole time?

Remember, either you are paying for college by working, or borrowing the money through loans, or your parents or generous donors—who have set up scholarship funds at your school—are paying for it for you. You might also be getting a break on your tuition due to a scholarship fund set up through taxpayers' dollars. You owe it to yourself, and to anyone who is helping pay for your education, to make the most of it. Imagine the following: Would you ever walk into the cafeteria, get ten different plates of food just so that you could try everything on the menu, eat only your favorite dish, and throw out the rest? Most people would not do this because it would be extremely wasteful. Withdrawing from *and* failing classes is much worse; figure out how much you or someone else (your family, scholarship donors, tax payers) paid for the class, and you will see that it is a huge waste of money—each failed class might be $3000 or more! Plus, each class you fail or withdraw from puts you behind.

Mistake 11: Failing to get a C or better in classes that require it. Be aware that some colleges require that you obtain at least a C in order to get credit for the class (you may have to earn an even higher grade in other classes). This most often applies to classes in your major, but it might also apply to general education classes like English. It is up to you to familiarize yourself with your school's policies. Legally, you cannot blame your advisor or the institution if you receive a C and fail to receive credit for the class. Ignorance of institutional policies (i.e., the "I didn't know!" defense) is not an excuse and will not result in the rules being changed. If you don't know the policies, you may graduate later, and at greater cost, than you intended.

Mistake 12: Taking only the minimum course load necessary to be classified as a full-time student. If you count up the number of credit hours needed to complete both your general education requirements and your major, you will see that you need to take *more* than the minimum number of hours each term in order to graduate on time. Taking the minimum number of credits, even for one term, may put you at risk for graduating in five years if your major has rigid credit-hour requirements.

Mistake 13: Asking for incompletes at the end of the term. Many schools will not let you take a grade of I (incomplete or in-progress) unless you have a medical excuse, are called oversees for military reasons, or have other similar circumstances. But some colleges will allow you to take an I at your discretion. If this is the case at your school, we recommend that you not do so. If you plan to finish coursework over winter break or over the summer, be aware that you run the risk of burning yourself out. Breaks are designed to give you a rest. It is also the time when your peers and family will be off having fun. Go ahead and finish, no matter how hard it is at the time, and do not leave the work until later. Most students find it extremely difficult to ever finish an incomplete course and are dismayed to find that the grade *automatically* turns into an F after a certain amount of time. Would you not rather have a C?

This chapter has provided you with guidance on graduating in four years, including information that many students are often left to discover on their own. Count yourself lucky! Now it is up to you to apply this wisdom. We motivate you to get the most out of your college experience by discussing why your grades matter; by providing tips on getting organized and making good impressions so that you will be able to make those good grades; and by discussing the importance of earning your grades honestly.

Glossary

Academic probation—the status of a student in danger of being dismissed from the university due to an unusually low grade point average.

Elective—any course that is not required by the general curriculum or by the major.

Financial aid package—scholarships, grants, loans, work-study positions, and other resources that are offered to a student as a package to make college affordable.

Fraternity—a selective all-male society devoted to networking, social activities, and charity work.

Grade forgiveness—a policy some schools have that allows students to retake a small number of classes for a better grade or to receive the average of the first and second attempts.

Nondisclosure agreement—a legal document stipulating that employees will not share specified information with other people or industries nor will employees create their own products (even on their own time) that are similar to products related to this employer (such a stipulation often lasts beyond one's time of employment).

Prerequisite—a lower-level university course that is required before taking a related upper-level course.

Registrar/registrar's office—the person/office that maintains student records and manages student registration.

Student loans—money loaned to students to pay for college expenses.

How Am I Expected to Perform in College?

5

This chapter surveys the ways in which grades and grading figure into your life as a college student. Making good grades in college is important for many reasons. Everything from your ability to play sports, to keeping a scholarship, to getting a professor's recommendation for a job or graduate program rests on your ability to perform well in your classes. Most freshmen do not understand that making the grade in college is completely different from making the grade in high school. Many of the tactics you employed in high school do not apply to higher education. We will also discuss how the **halo effect**, or making a good first impression, can improve your chances for better grades in your classes. We will conclude with a frank discussion about ethics, academic integrity, and the ramifications of cheating in order to make the grade.

Does My GPA Really Matter?
THE IMPORTANCE OF GRADES

When surveyed at the beginning of a course, most students report that they expect to earn an A in the course. That is a great goal, but it may not be realized. By the end of each term, only a select number of students actually earn an A. One reason for this discrepancy is that some people overestimate their abilities in handling the material, in juggling other responsibilities, and in time management. Freshmen, in particular, are used to the grade inflation of high school, where extra credit and other approaches sometimes guarantee high grades. Another reason that students plan to get an A but ultimately do not is that students begin each term with the best intentions but get caught up in general college life. If you are failing to get high grades due to college life, it is time to get serious. Your

Professor Sheryl Hartman, Ph.D.

Image courtesy of Miami Dade College - North Campus

From Session 5 of *College Orientation*, First Edition. Karen Bendersky, Catherine M. Chastain-Elliott.

grades do matter. But *why* do grades matter? There is a short-term answer and a long-term answer to this question.

What Is the Importance of My Grades in the Short Term?

In the short term, if you have a scholarship, your grades can affect whether or not you can keep it. You need to maintain a certain grade point average in order to retain scholarships. Do what it takes to keep your scholarship. Paying for college is expensive, so a scholarship should be taken seriously. You are lucky to have a scholarship. Because *you* have it, someone else *does not* have it. In other words, you have a moral obligation to take getting good grades seriously. Someone without that scholarship may have desperately needed it and perhaps would have appreciated it more.

We also want to communicate why you should never beg for a grade from a professor or pressure him or her for the grade you want. It is unethical for your professor to give a grade that you have not earned. A faculty member will not respond to a student who tries to guilt him or her into changing a grade, because the belief at the university level is that grades should reflect the quality of the work.

Many students try to keep up their GPA by withdrawing from courses in which they are performing poorly. Unfortunately this is a bad practice for two reasons. First, some universities limit the number of withdrawals—Ws—that are allowed on your transcript. Once you accumulate a certain number of Ws, all subsequent withdrawals may be recorded as WF (withdraw/failing, which is essentially an F; check your university's policy). Unless you experienced a serious personal situation and can document it (for instance, you coped with mononucleosis one term), these Ws and WFs are red flags to hiring committees and graduate schools. They may keep you ·from getting the job, or getting into the postgraduate program, that you want. Think about the messages a W sends: This is the type of student who gives up easily, who does not challenge him or herself, and who would rather take easy courses. Before you drop a class, try to determine why you are having difficulty and address the problem. See a tutor, if necessary, or make an appointment at the counseling center if you are facing other difficulties. Try to better your grade, even if you realize it is your own fault—if you have been slacking off, for instance, and are now very far behind. And remember, withdrawing from classes adds to the total number of terms you spend in school, which can become costly.

A high GPA will gain you admittance to select undergraduate **honor societies** and groups. Examples include the academic national honor society Phi Kappa Phi, and many subject- and campus-leadership-related honor societies. Once you are a member of these groups, you will be eligible for special grants, scholarships, fellowships, and awards offered through these organizations. These grants, scholarships, and fellowships might help pay for your tuition costs or for your books, or they may help pay for summer study or research. These groups also often offer money for graduate study.

Being a member of honor societies will also look good on your résumé; it shows that you are a hard worker and an achiever.

Likewise, a low GPA will affect your academic standing within the university. If you drop below a certain GPA, often a 2.0, you may be placed on academic probation. If you do not raise your GPA within a set time period, the university may expel you. Typically, poor grades are the result of a lack of focus or commitment to school; poor grades rarely relate to ability.

What Is the Importance of My Grades in the Long Term?

A record number of people are attending college. As a result, it is getting more and more difficult to obtain jobs and gain admittance to graduate schools. You will somehow need to stand out from the pack. One new tactic job seekers are using is listing their GPA on the education section of their résumé. To do so yourself, you should have a GPA that looks competitive. What is a competitive GPA? It is one that is at least 3.5, because that average communicates that you are an A student. Otherwise, do not list it. Try to keep your grades up so you can compete with the other job and graduate school candidates.

Regarding graduate school, it is difficult to gain admittance to most programs. Some people mistakenly believe that since they were able to get into college with a so-so academic record that they will automatically be accepted to a graduate program. This is not the case. Graduate schools accept only *strong* students and doctorate programs accept only *exceptional* students. In general, there are many more applicants to graduate school than there are open spaces. Take a clinical psychology program, for example. Most programs admit an average of ten students a year. This same program might receive close to 200 applications for those ten spots. What criteria will they use to evaluate the applicants? GPA will certainly be one of them.

Graduate schools, and increasingly businesses, will request a copy of your college transcript. They want to verify your résumé and see what classes you have taken. They will also examine your grade trends. Are you a consistently good student who took a heavy course load or are you a student who could earn only decent grades if you had a light schedule (around 12 or fewer hours per term)? Again, they will also notice any Ws (withdrawals) and will pay attention to grades of D and F.

It is very important to keep your grades up—both in the short and the long term. Do not automatically eliminate your chances for certain opportunities in life by getting bad grades.

Why Am I Always Tired?
THE IMPORTANCE OF TIME MANAGEMENT

Using your time effectively is a key skill for both college and life after graduation. Some come to college with amazing time-management skills, others learn along the way, and then there are those who stubbornly refuse to get organized. Luckily, attending college is unique because you get a fresh start every new term. Keep this in mind as you move through your college years and use it to your advantage. The only time you will have a similar opportunity once you graduate is when you switch jobs or change your career. You have complete control over how you approach or whether you engage in time management, even if you have an established pattern that you know is not the best. Every new term is an opportunity to reconsider what you normally do. If your typical pattern works, great, stick with it. If it does not, only *you* can change it. Your family and your instructors cannot force you to be organized, nor will the best organizational tools work for you if you never use them. In this section, we offer sound advice on what we know works.

Why Use a Calendar?

Managing your time essentially means tracking it, and it can be made much easier by organizing your commitments into just a few main categories: Courses, Work, Social Activities, Other. Your first priority every term is obtaining a calendar. The second is filling it in with obligations related to your courses. Course obligations include attending classes and scheduling time for studying, writing, projects, and meetings. Remember, depending on your familiarity with course material, you need to schedule from one to four hours of study time for *every* hour you spend in class. Next, fill in your work schedule (making adjustments *around* your course related times). Only then should you add in your social and other obligations. Good time management begins with scheduling your courses because at typical four-year schools, your professors expect this to be your priority. Get a calendar, either paper or electronic, and fill it in completely at the beginning of each term.

Why Use the Course Syllabus?

The course syllabus is an invaluable time-management tool. The syllabus is a summary document that orients students to the course and its expectations. Using it is the first step toward a successful learning experience. The syllabus contains crucial information on the organizational structure of the course topics that will assist you in studying for the course and understanding the material. It also will list the instructor's contact information (e.g., teaching assistants, office hours, office location/s, and means of contact) should you need to seek additional assistance. In general, the syllabus should be treated as your first tool toward performing well in any class.

We offer the following list of steps on how to use your syllabus as a time-management tool. Not all steps may be needed for your particular set-up and personality. Make a habit of doing the following the first week of class (these will be helpful, especially if you are disorganized or a procrastinator):

1. **Read the entire syllabus.** Most instructors spend the first day of class just going through it. Do not miss this class. It is legally assumed that you accept everything listed on that syllabus when you stay in a course. This means that even if you unwittingly violate a syllabus policy (because you never read it closely), you are still held accountable. For instance, you might find yourself automatically dropped from a class after two absences. You can claim ignorance, but it will *not* get you back in the course.

2. **Bookmark the websites listed on the syllabus.** The use of websites tied to courses (such as Blackboard©, or Turnitin.com©) is becoming ubiquitous. You want to be sure you have access to these sites and understand how to use them. Even if you use a specific site every term, there is no guarantee that your name is on the access list once a new term begins. You want to check this early just in case you need to contact the instructor, or campus technology support, about it. The last thing you want is to find out that you cannot access a posted assignment that is due in a couple of hours (and it is way too late to contact the instructor). Similarly, you will want to know what upload formats (.pdf, .txt, .doc, .rtf, or .odt) are accepted by certain sites well before an assignment is due.

3. **Create a hard copy of your syllabus.** Some syllabi are available only online. We recommend printing a hard copy for your records. You do not want to find yourself in the situation when you really need your syllabus but the Internet is not available.

4. **Keep your syllabus copy in a safe place.** For some students, this is the note-taking book that they use for the class. If this is the case for you, be sure it is secured in this notebook (e.g., in a flap or actually snapped into a three-ring binder). Do not just fold it and slip it into the pages where it can easily fall out. Others might opt to have a separate folder used just for course handouts. Choose what works for you.

5. **Record your entire course schedule into your weekly calendar.** This is admittedly tedious (try using an online calendar for ease), but do it. We know that you will probably have your course schedule memorized by the end of the first week, but every now and then you may forget where you are supposed to be. At least this way, you can look at your calendar. More importantly, if you have your course *inked* into your calendar you will think twice before scheduling another activity over it. Hopefully, you will at least pause to think, "Is this activity really worth missing this class?" Please, don't do it.

6. **Transfer all course requirement due dates into your weekly calendar.** This is a must do. This is the only way to keep up with scheduled exams and quizzes and with paper and assignment due dates. Yes, some instructors give reminders in class, but not all do. Also, what if you miss the class in which the instructor gives the reminder? As both students and professors, we have personally witnessed students who have shown up for class completely unaware that something was due, or worse, that it was exam day.

7. **Create a course-management spreadsheet.** For those courses in which the professor does not use an online course-management system (e.g., Blackboard©) you should transfer the course's requirements (e.g., quizzes, tests, papers, or assignments) into a spreadsheet so you can keep a record of your earned grades/scores. You can also jot these scores down next to each listed course requirement on your hard copy syllabus, but it is better to create a course spreadsheet (whether electronic or a paper version). The spreadsheet also provides a single place for all your grade monitoring. Use the first spreadsheet column to list the course's requirements. Then add a column for the number of points (or highest grade) possible for each requirement and another column for the points (or grade) that you actually earned.

Why Use a Mid-Term Checkup?

At mid-term, consult your course-requirement spreadsheet. You will know exactly how you are doing so far and have a sense of whether you need to seek additional help (your grades are lower than you would like) or get yourself in gear (you see that you have lots of zeros listed, or nothing entered at all).

Performing as you had wanted is your goal. If you are not meeting this goal, take time to consider why. If the issue is too much of a social life, then it is clear that you need to cut back. Look at your calendar: Are your social obligations trumping your course obligations? If the issue is that some social life issues are too much to handle, then it is definitely time to visit the counseling center. Common social issues may include roommate problems, romantic partner problems, drinking, group commitment pressures, and family commitment pressures. Maybe you have a solid calendar and are sticking to it faithfully but still not making the grade. Could something else be wrong? In this case, you probably are experiencing course learning-related issues. Perhaps you need to change your study technique (rather than how much you are studying). Maybe you just need additional academic guidance. In this case, we recommend talking with your course instructor and visiting the appropriate tutoring center or lab. Whatever the case, we encourage you to use your campus's resources to help.

What Are the Warning Signs That I Am Doing Too Much?

The following is a list of signs that suggest you are doing too much. Read the list and see if more than two or three of them apply to you. Keep in mind that you might be able to engage in all of your chosen activities if you simply schedule them appropriately. Our suggestion is to first identify whether you are in danger of foundering by using this list and then reassess how you schedule your time. Did you make a calendar? Did you really add *all* of your college components (courses, work, social activities, other) into this calendar? If the answer is no, give it a try. It can only help.

▷*Are You . . .*

1. giving excuses to your professors?
2. asking professors for special considerations?
3. always tired?
4. getting low exam grades?
5. skipping classes?
6. getting sick often?
7. withdrawing from classes?
8. not keeping up with assignments?
9. doing assignments at the last minute?

If you are experiencing more than two to three of these warning signs and you are sticking to your calendar, you may need to decrease your involvement with extracurricular activities. Your academic performance and your health are in danger.

What Do I Need to Know about Working While in College?

We certainly do not want to discourage anyone from seeking a four-year degree, but we have seen our share of students who flounder, drop out, or take double the time (and money) to finish because they were juggling too many roles. We have had students who have done it all, and done it all well, but they are the exception—and they are exceptional. They perform at the top of the class, have perfect attendance, never make excuses, and never miss an exam or assignment. They are masters of time management! Unless you are this type of student, we suggest that you work no more than ten hours per week while in school. If you must work more—for instance, if you are a mature adult supporting a family—practice good time management and use your calendar as previously outlined. Additionally, have a backup plan ready for those times when you have to deal with extra stress or unexpected problems. For some students, this is a family member who can take over when necessary, an alternative daycare option, or a class peer you trust to take excellent notes and never miss class. You might also schedule a time cushion between your workdays and school days so the two will never overlap. When you graduate and obtain a career-path job, your supervisor might not be willing to make special arrangements for your other obligations and so it is important that you get in the habit of having a backup plan ready. If you need help deciding how much you should (or need to) work, consider meeting with a campus advisor or even a counselor and discussing your situation with them. They can assist you in making the best decision (being a full-time or part-time student) given your specific situation.

⟩ *Should I Work While in College? (Check all boxes that apply.)*

> ☐ I plan to work fewer than ten hours per week.
>
> ☐ I regularly use a daily planner or smart phone calendar.
>
> ☐ I schedule all aspects of my life (work, class, studying, and social time).
>
> ☐ I will quit or lower my work hours if my grades begin to suffer.
>
> ☐ I will not ask my professors to accommodate my work schedule.
>
> ☐ I will not miss class due to my work schedule.
>
> ☐ I work to build up my résumé or to help pay school expenses.

If you did not check off all of the options, think twice about working. Full-time students who work more than ten hours per week are often stressed, make excuses for their poor class performance, and frequently ask for special arrangements to accommodate their work schedules. They are often in danger of taking more than four years to graduate.

Am I Making a Good Impression?
WHAT YOU NEED TO KNOW ABOUT THE HALO EFFECT

The halo effect, also known as the importance of making a good first impression, is established early. The halo is created when the first impression you make on professors is being a student who is interested, interesting, intelligent, thoughtful, respectful, timely, mature, and well organized. In other words, they think you are a great student and reward you accordingly because you act like one, especially at the beginning of the term (i.e., you attend class and are punctual, ask thoughtful questions, submit quality work, and generally have a good attitude). The halo effect occurs when you make a mistake or botch something at a later time. For instance, you miss an exam and want to make it up. The professor is more likely to be accommodating if you have the halo. He or she will think, "This is a good student. I'm sure he did everything he could to try and take this exam on time. I'll go ahead and give him the same exam as everyone else, because this guy wouldn't cheat." For a student without the halo, the professor thinks, "He's done nothing all term and suddenly he wants me to bend over backward for him. Well that's not happening. I'm not even sure that I trust his excuse for missing the exam. I'm not letting him make the exam up." In general, people are more willing to give you the benefit of the doubt if they have a good impression of you. It is easier for you to make the grade, both literally and metaphorically, if you present yourself well at the outset. This is true both in college and in the work place. In both, you should try to earn your halo early. It is almost impossible to make up for a terrible first impression.

Image courtesy of Miami Dade College - North Campus

It's Not My Major, So What's the Big Deal?
ETHICAL BEHAVIOR AND ACADEMIC INTEGRITY

As important as good grades are, it is vitally important that you *earn* them. Cheating has consequences that you may never have considered. In this section, we discuss the importance of ethical behavior and academic integrity. We will discuss the real cost of cheating to individuals and society; what happens on college and university campuses when you get caught cheating; and finally, **plagiarism** (intentionally or unintentionally representing someone else's ideas or words as your own), proper **citing** (crediting a source for their ideas or writing), and the plagiarism-detection software called Turnitin.com.

What Is the Real Cost of Cheating?

Recently, an extended family out for Sunday brunch was overheard discussing grades with the college-aged adults among them. A professor who was sitting at the very next table perked up as the conversation began and thought, "how wonderful—if only more families would talk about the pitfalls of cheating." Then the conversation took an unexpected turn. One of the parents laughed and said, "But you know, what's the old saying . . . 'It's better to cheat than to repeat.'" The professor was dismayed. But he continued to listen and heard another adult say, "Yes, but if you get caught, the consequences can be bad, so you don't want to cheat and get caught!"

The problem with cheating is not getting caught—it is the act of cheating itself. When one cheats, one's win is someone else's loss. It is increasingly clear that cheating is on the rise, even at the country's most selective institutions. The situation of an Ivy League student caught plagiarizing passages of a book made the news in recent years. Also in the news, a school was profiled for deciding to allow plagiarism; it is so easy to cut and paste from the Internet, the argument went, and so hard to monitor, that plagiarizing should no longer be seen as cheating. Students should make the grade for simply locating information online. While we can understand not wanting to be left behind when others get ahead by cheating, even a little cheating ultimately affects individuals and society in some very real and costly ways.

What are some of the specific ramifications of cheating? First, while cheating may provide short-term gratification (for instance, an A on an assignment), it can diminish your overall happiness. Self-esteem, or your self-worth, is a key component of life satisfaction. Self-esteem comes only from working hard and earning your worth. Dishonest behavior adds up. Even if you get away with cheating, doing so can cause you to doubt, dislike, and ultimately lose respect for yourself. Over time, you will begin to attribute your abilities to others (those off of whom you cheat), not to yourself. In a stressful situation you will find yourself thinking, "I need to cheat. I can't do this on my own." When you enter the working world and the manager wants you to write a ten-page report on the latest initiative—by the end of what may be a very busy week—you will not have anyone or anything to cheat off of. You will lack the confidence, and the ability, to do the work. In school, the harder you work, the better you feel about yourself and your life, even if you do not always get A's. You will always know that you "gave it the old college try." Work hard and conduct your affairs honestly. Ethical behavior adds up later to confidence at work and happiness in life.

Second, consider how cheaters potentially hurt the honest students in a class. Imagine the following scenario. A sociology professor sits down to grade a set of research papers. He is going along, paper by paper, thinking that this time around, the papers seem to be very average. Students are showing a clear weakness demonstrating mastery over the finer points of the discipline's citation style. The professor says to himself, "Hmmm . . . I must not have covered the citation style as thoroughly in this section as in my other section . . . I think I will bump everyone's grade up five points, and discuss citing in greater depth on Tuesday." Then he gets to your paper, that you downloaded from the Internet A-paper database. The citations are in perfect form. The professor then says to himself, "Great paper! I guess I *did* cover citing in class and only one person was paying attention." He then decides *not* to add the five points to everyone else's papers. These students all get lower grades. Moreover, the professor never goes over citing again with the class, as he had planned. As a result, this group of sociology majors remains weak in the area of citation for several terms to come; they lose additional points in their advanced classes because their professors think they should have mastered citation format at the lower levels. Thus, when you cheat, you steal from others. You literally steal their points and their opportunity to learn. Always remember that a dishonest action you take can affect others—and for more than one term. Do you really want to be part of a situation like this?

Consider also how cheaters can affect their classmates later on, when they are trying to land graduate school acceptances or jobs. Professors write letters of recommendations for graduate programs and act as references for jobs. What if we recommend a habitual cheater who never got caught as an undergraduate, but who gets caught cheating in graduate school or at work—where the stakes are much higher? Our recommendation for that school and workplace becomes null and void. For example, you might want to get into a certain graduate program, but since the last student we recommended to that same graduate program was caught being dishonest, our recommendation will not be taken seriously. Similarly, when a workplace views your résumé and, seeing our name as a reference, realizes that the last person we recommended had honesty issues, they will simply not contact you.

Finally, contemplate the idea that people who cheat in small ways often go on to cheat in big ways. "White collar cheating" among adults in America is rampant. The **chief financial officer** (CFO, the highest finance position in a company) misreports a company's earnings and artificially inflates the cost of its stock shares. A politician spends campaign funds illegally on personal luxuries. An accountant embezzles company funds. Cheating is kind of like going off of a diet, if you will, with the diet being honest behavior, and sneaking a full-fat dessert being cheating. Once you justify a single dessert (or copying the answers from someone's take-home worksheet), it becomes easier and easier to do it again, and suddenly, you are not just sneaking desserts, you are no longer on a diet at all. You are eating whatever you want—or cheating "big time," to finish the analogy. Remember: *Everything* becomes easier with practice, including dishonest behavior. So do not let yourself even start.

Professor Sheryl Hartman, Ph.D.

Image courtesy of Miami Dade College - North Campus

What Happens If I Get Caught Cheating?

So what happens if you cheat and get caught? You need to know the consequences. Cheating is handled differently at different institutions, but none of the methods are pleasant. Perhaps the most common (and unpleasant) procedure is being required to attend an academic integrity hearing in which a group of faculty and students hears the professor's side of the story, your side of the story, and then decides on a punishment. (Be aware that the students chosen to participate are usually excellent students and often recommend harsher punishment than the faculty members.) Getting let off entirely is rare; a point score of zero on the assignment in question is considered to be a light punishment; an F in the entire course for an offense that you might consider to be mild is extremely common; and getting kicked out of your school generally occurs when the incident is your second or third offense, or if what you did was egregious. Several years ago, one of the authors sat in on a student integrity hearing and remembers not batting an eyelash when she agreed, with the others, that a cheating student be expelled. The student's pleas that this was the only school for her and that she thought she was a valuable asset to the volleyball team, did not win her favor. She had submitted two research papers at the same time in one class, both of which were plagiarized. Each plagiarized paper counted as a separate cheating incident. Two cheating incidents at the school were grounds for expulsion.

Most schools permanently note **academic integrity violations** (a breach of your school's academic integrity/cheating guidelines) on student transcripts, which follow you for life and may affect your ability to start again at another school, get the job you want, or get into a graduate program. Some universities keep a list of cheaters. This list includes all students who have violated their campus's honor code—or honest behavior policy—and it may be consulted when professors suspect dishonesty. Professors can check the list if they have doubts about a student's integrity in class (for example, regarding an excuse for being absent), and make an informed decision. Like it or not, professors also talk with each other about you and your cheating behavior. We sometimes know of cheaters' reputations before they even take a class with us. Such students have missed the halo effect and will not receive the benefit of the doubt. Saying that you did not know, did not understand, or did not intend to cheat will not help you and will in fact make the situation worse. Neither will saying that your school has a "culture of cheating" or that "everybody's doing it" help your situation. You are better off to admit an offense and genuinely apologize for your actions. The fact of the matter is that it is getting easier and easier to cheat due to technology, pressure from students who have been allowed to get away with cheating at the secondary school level, and pressure from parents who threaten lawsuits when their children are found guilty of cheating. As a consequence, professors are hypervigilant about cheating.

What Do I Need to Know about Plagiarism, Citing, and Turnitin.com?

Plagiarism is the most common form of cheating, but all forms of cheating pose serious academic integrity violations. Plagiarism involves claiming someone else's ideas as your own, or their phrasing, sentences, paragraphs, or entire documents as your own. People deserve credit for both their ideas and for the hard work they put into the actual writing they produce to convey their ideas. In general, to avoid plagiarism, you must state where you got your information. You must do so when you introduce ideas that you did not come up with yourself, when you copy more than two words in a row (excluding "a," "an" or "the"), when you quote a source directly (or word for word, using quote marks at the beginning and end of what you copy into your own paper), and when you **paraphrase**—or put into your own words—whole sections of a document. You can even plagiarize yourself, known as **self-plagiarism**. This occurs when you copy your *own* work submitted some place else (another class, another journal, or another blog) and submit it somewhere different as if it is a new work. In the professional realm, this would happen if you submitted the same published work to a different publisher. In college, you might submit an old paper of yours to a different course. Both examples are considered plagiarism because they entail duplication of a work (even if it is your own). Neither act helps the topic field or the student.

A common complaint from students is that they cannot think of another way to say something other than the way they initially found it, and so they quote long passages unnecessarily. (Quoting should be reserved for highlighting noteworthy phrases or passages.) There is always another way to say something, and you will be able to do so with practice. With all the writing you will be asked to do in college, you will master this skill, if you apply yourself, by the time you are a senior. To help you get started, take a best effort draft of your next writing assignment to your college's writing center.

Once you present ideas that are not your own, quote a document or a person, rephrase an idea, or paraphrase a document, how do you cite the information? There are several standard formats, or styles, for citing your sources. Be prepared for your professors to be particular about which format is appropriate for their academic discipline. As a college-level learner, you will be required to become skilled at more than one citation style, each of which requires a specific reference-noting system. Reference notes may appear in parentheses within the text, at the bottom of each page as footnotes, or at the end of your paper as endnotes. Using word-processing software, the writer controls the placement of the notes and citation characteristics, such as whether or not to use Roman or Arabic numerals. Your professor will grade you on the degree to which you learn and follow the parameters of the assigned style guidelines. Visit your college or university's writing center if you need help citing your work.

Finally on the matter of plagiarism, you need to know about turnitin.com and other tools now available to identify cheating. Educate yourself about these tools. Turnitin.com is an online service that specifically reviews students' submitted papers for plagiarism. This site works by archiving (warehousing) all uploaded papers and then generating an originality report for each student's submitted work. With a click of the mouse, your instructor can see what percentage of your written work corresponds or exactly matches another, and by how much. This tool is extremely popular because it not only compares your work to your current classmates', but also compares it with all work that has ever been submitted at all other schools. Not only that, it compares the information you wrote to information found on other websites (like Wikipedia). Professors use these tools for two reasons:

1. as a guide for measuring whether students understand what plagiarism entails, and

2. to root out dishonest people so that the majority of students, the noncheaters, can be fairly assessed.

In this chapter, we have focused on grades—why they matter in both the short term and the long term. We have also covered why managing time is essential to making the grade and why it is crucial to you, to your classmates, and ultimately, to society at large to obtain grades honestly. Cultivating the personal habit of integrity is one of the most significant life skills that the college experience can offer you. Meet the challenge by examining your own actions, and do the right thing at every opportunity.

Now we will examine your life beyond the classroom. One of the most exciting things about college is the fact that something always seems to be happening around you. We will explain how college has the potential to enrich you, and to provide you with additional life skills, outside the academic arena.

Glossary

Academic integrity violation—a breach of your school's academic integrity guidelines; cheating.

CFO—chief financial officer, the highest finance position in a company.

Citing—openly and purposefully giving due credit to a source for their ideas or writing.

Halo effect—a person's good first impression that quells later doubt by a superior.

Honor society—any selective society that recognizes students who have achieved academically and/or in leadership roles on campus.

Paraphrase—to summarize someone else's ideas or words by putting them into your own words; citation, or acknowledging one's source, is required when paraphrasing.

Plagiarism—intentionally or unintentionally representing someone else's ideas or words as your own.

Self-plagiarism—duplicating your own previous work and representing it as new work.

6 Time Management

Pouring her fourth cup of coffee at 11:00 P.M., Laura searched for the history paper assignment that her professor had handed out a month ago. It was due at 9:00 A.M. tomorrow, and she was just getting started.

Laura sank into her chair at the kitchen table to go through her backpack one more time and debated whether to call a classmate for help. Was it too late to call? She sent a text to Michael, a classmate who always seemed to be organized, and waited for his response.

Laura didn't normally procrastinate about her schoolwork, but her youngest child had been sick for two days and she had been at home caring for him. She also wasn't sure what topic to write about in her paper. When Michael had sent a message three days ago that he'd completed the paper, she hadn't worried too much about her ability to get it done.

After three hours of intense work, Laura finished the paper. It wasn't perfect, but it was the required "at least eight pages in length" and on topic. Her eyes were too tired to proofread the paper after finishing it, but she decided to print it out before going to bed.

"I hope Professor Mallick doesn't read these papers very carefully," Laura said to herself as she began printing out the paper. Then the loud screech of the printer got her attention! She knew the screech meant that she wouldn't be able to print out and review her paper at home. She'd have to go to campus early and try to find a working printer before her class. Right now, she just wanted to get a couple hours of sleep.

As you read Laura's story, you probably picked up on the key idea that a lot of the stress she's facing about her assignment is due to her own procrastination and lack of planning. As you step into college, you may face similar challenges.

To help you become a better time manager, this chapter will help you learn how to do the following:

- Develop an effective time-management strategy.
- Prioritize your activities.
- Make the best use of various time-management tools.
- Avoid common time-management pitfalls.

LEARNING OUTCOME

Create an academic time-management plan.

MyStudentSuccessLab (www.mystudentsuccesslab.com) is an online solution designed to help you 'Start strong, Finish stronger' by building skills for ongoing personal and professional development.

NOW IS THE TIME TO DEVELOP AN EFFECTIVE TIME-MANAGEMENT STRATEGY

The number-one issue that college students say is their biggest challenge is time management. Why?

- **The college experience adds new and different responsibilities to an already busy life.** Even before you stepped onto campus, you probably felt like your life was busy. Now, you are going to college full time on top of having a full-time life.

- **The college experience brings high expectations.** As a highly motivated, success-oriented person, you have already placed high expectations on yourself. Now, in addition to your own expectations, your professors, advisors, parents, and other people who care about you will have expectations for you to succeed.

- **The college experience includes a wide variety of responsibilities.** As a full-time student, you're taking three to five different classes—each with its own requirements and schedule. You may also be involved in clubs or other student organizations and working and juggling family and social responsibilities, as well.

- **The college experience puts you in charge.** You have far more autonomy to make decisions about how you spend your time in college than you did previously in high school or at work. Having this freedom can be exciting, but it also brings a new level of responsibility for managing your time without direct supervision from your parents, teachers, or employer.

To face the time-management challenge, you need to develop an effective time-management strategy. An effective strategy will help you be productive (get a lot done), effective (do it well), and satisfied (feel good about it) in your personal and academic lives.

One of the main reasons having an effective time-management strategy helps you feel satisfied is that it helps you feel in control. As explained by Nelson and Low (2010, pp. 100–101) in their book about emotional intelligence, "An important by-product of good time management is a feeling of self-control—we are managing our responsibilities, not being managed by them." You will certainly feel more in control of your time after you complete this chapter!

Your time-management strategy is your plan for using your most valuable resource—your time—to fulfill your personal mission statement and to achieve your goals (SMART goals, of course!). How you use your time and organize your activities will depend on your goals (such as completing your degree, securing a job, and building relationships) and your personal mission statement (which defines your values and purpose in life). For example, if your personal mission statement places a high level of importance on helping others and giving back to society, then your allocation of time to activities that reflect those values should be consistent.

Throughout this chapter, be sure to keep your goals and mission statement in sight, as they should serve as the compass that guides your time-management decisions.

KNOW YOUR PRIORITIES

You may already have some kind of system for keeping track of all the various tasks you have to complete, activities you need to attend, and people you need to contact. Items like these typically end up on your to-do list or a scattered selection of sticky notes posted around your dorm room or car interior.

Meeting EXPECTATIONS

The college will expect that I ...	To meet that expectation, I will ...
Example: . . . *turn in assignments on time.*	Example: . . . *post assignments on my calendar system as soon as I get them and schedule blocks of time on my calendar well before assignment due dates to start working on them.*

You also know from experience that not every responsibility or activity on your list is of equal importance. To be successful in school and in life, you need to focus on the most important (and not necessarily the most urgent) responsibilities and activities.

Some responsibilities and activities might be urgent but not important, while others may be important but not urgent. An urgent responsibility or activity tries to demand your time and energy right now. For instance, suppose that your friends are texting you to make plans for the evening, and they want you to reply right away. But at the moment, you're devoting your attention to developing long-term goals and writing a personal mission statement. What should you do: reply to the text message or keep working?

Making this decision requires distinguishing between the urgent and the important—something you do hundreds of times every day. The more you keep your focus on achieving what's important and keeping what's urgent within manageable limits, the more success you will experience.

Distinguishing between the urgent and the important will help you engage in an important activity: prioritizing. A *priority* is something that is important and urgent at the moment. *Prioritizing* is the act of ranking or sorting responsibilities and activities from most important to least important to help you decide what to do, at what time, and what to work on first.

As you step into the college experience, the number of activities and responsibilities competing for your time and attention will quickly multiply. Your ability to prioritize will be critically important to your success. You will need to continually review the list of activities and responsibilities in your life and keep them ranked according to their importance.

Here's an example of a prioritization strategy you may want to try. Look at the syllabus from one of the classes you're taking this semester, and find the "Grading" section. Professors typically provide information about how

It's in the SYLLABUS

Look at the syllabus for each course you're taking to help determine your priorities and tasks for each week of the semester. Record the due dates for all of your assignments in all of your classes in a single calendar system. Chances are, deadlines will overlap some weeks, and you'll find yourself needing to take an exam and finish a project in the same week. By planning ahead, you can work on some of these assignments ahead of time, thereby avoiding having to complete several important projects at once. Also think about these questions:

- How much time do you anticipate spending on each course?
- What days or weeks will be particularly busy for you?
- What additional obligations will you have during those busy times?
- How will you manage your priorities and time?

they will determine grades in their classes, including percentages or point values of individual assignments, quizzes, exams, and projects that make up a student's total grade. For instance, the final exam in your calculus course might account for 25% of your grade, whereas one of the quizzes might be worth 3%. Which of these two is most important? Clearly, because the final exam contributes far more to your grade than an individual quiz, the exam is more important (assuming that you're looking at the issue primarily in terms of your grade). Comparing individual assignments, projects, and exams on the basis of their value or contribution to your total grade is one useful technique that can help you prioritize your work.

Deadlines, of course, are another important consideration in prioritizing. In general, an assignment or responsibility that has an immediate deadline should be a higher priority than one that's due later. But also be sure to differentiate between the urgent and the important. If you focus only on those responsibilities that have near-term deadlines, then you won't have much time to work on activities that are more important, such as setting long-term goals and conducting research to help you plan your career. One approach to meeting this challenge is to give yourself a fixed amount of time each day to tackle the urgent issues in your life, while also scheduling time for important but not urgent activities.

USING TOOLS CAN HELP YOU MANAGE TIME

As you implement your time-management strategy, you can draw on a wide variety of tools to help you achieve your goals.

Calendars, Lists, and Workspaces

If you prefer to use a paper calendar, you have several different types to choose from: daily, weekly, and monthly. Once you determine the type that works best for you, make a habit of writing down the tasks you need to do, no matter how big or small. Here's an example of a typical list of a day's activities for a student like Laura:

Thursday
- Make appointment to have oil changed.
- Pick up medicine for Mom.
- Turn in housing deposit for next semester.
- Study for history quiz on Friday.
- Write essay for English composition.
- Turn in student club membership application.

A typical monthly calendar allows you to see several weeks at once, so that you can be aware of upcoming events. Often, however, there is little space on a monthly calendar to write down detailed information, such as Laura's activity list.

A weekly calendar allows you to glance at one week at a time. The key benefit of a weekly calendar is that it gives you room to write out the details of specific activities. However, a key drawback of a weekly calendar is that you won't be able to look ahead at what you have to do in the next week or two.

A daily calendar usually provides the most space to write day-to-day tasks and appointments. This kind of calendar may be the most difficult to work with, though, if you need to plan ahead. Since you can't see the rest of the week or month, you may overlook important events or be surprised by them. Use a daily calendar if you are extremely organized and can plan ahead effectively, or use it in addition to a monthly calendar.

If you have reliable Internet access in your home, apartment, or dorm, and access to a computer while on campus, consider using a web-based electronic calendar system and priority list. Also consider using your phone's calendar to help you stay on track. In many cases, your phone calendar can be synced to your computer calendar, which will allow you to stay updated no matter what device or devices you use. An electronic calendar allows you to set up events to automatically repeat themselves (for example, "Calculus quiz every Thursday"; "Dad's birthday on March 18"), to revise priority lists without having to rewrite them, to set up reminders and alerts that prompt you about upcoming deadlines and events, and to share your calendar with others so you can coordinate team projects and family responsibilities. The added benefit of a web-based system is that you can access it anytime and anywhere you have Internet access.

Once you've chosen the calendar system that works best for you, find your university's academic calendar on the campus website or in the catalog, and add the following important dates to your schedule:

Checklist of Important Dates
_____ Deadlines for registering and filing financial aid forms
_____ Date for the beginning of classes (or instruction)
_____ Drop/add dates for changing class schedule
_____ Due dates for paying tuition and fees
_____ Withdrawal dates for leaving college before semester is over
_____ Registration dates for next semester
_____ Holidays or breaks within the semester and between semesters

Deciding on the ideal calendar and creating a priority list are the first steps to managing your time well, but there is more you can do. Creating a quiet, clutter-free space where you can study and complete assignments will also help you manage your time effectively and efficiently. If you don't have a place in your house or apartment that you can call your own, try to set up a comfortable chair at the kitchen table. Make sure your workspace is comfortable and quiet and has adequate space for books, notebooks, and other supplies. It has to be a place that you want to be, or you will find it difficult to go there and stay on task.

Routines Are Time-Management Tools

Once you've set up an effective calendar and priority list, you can start to establish a time-management routine that helps you stay on track and maintain control over your life. For your calendar and task list to be effective, you need to establish the daily routine of reviewing and updating this information. Take a few minutes every evening to review what you've accomplished and to check off those items from your priority list (this will be a very satisfying experience!), to add new tasks that come up during the day, and to review tomorrow's calendar and priority list so you can anticipate tomorrow's goals.

Knowing what to expect during the day will make surprises less likely. Also, if you know that you have an early start tomorrow, you can make special preparations the night

THE UNWRITTEN RULES

Of Time Management

- **Projects, papers, and exams all tend to collide at the same time each term.** The best way not only to survive but also to succeed each term is to start early on your projects and assignments. Also be sure to review your notes and class materials each week so that studying for midterms and finals won't require as much time or effort.

- **The best times to accomplish important items on your priority list may come between terms.** Look for opportunities during spring break, holiday breaks, summer, and even three-day weekends to enjoy some peace and quiet and to revisit the important-but-not-urgent items on your list (for example, your personal mission statement, SMART goals, and career plan).

- **No matter how well you think you can work under pressure, your professors will detect procrastination.** As soon as a professor sees

evidence of your procrastination, you'll be at a disadvantage. Most important, if you wait too long to start or complete an assignment, you'll forego the biggest advantage of getting an early start: the opportunity to get helpful feedback from your professor on preliminary drafts of your work. According to Beck (2012), "Too much stress, fatigue, and time pressure can kill creativity: A little bit of stress might help to get you motivated, but too much of it will typically cause you to shut down."

- **Even with today's technology, it takes time to learn.** In a comprehensive study of student success, chronicled in the book *What Matters in College*, Astin (1997) notes that the amount of time students spend practicing what they are trying to learn (or "time on task") is *the* single greatest predictor of academic success. Sorry, no shortcuts here!

before, such as packing your lunch, organizing your backpack, looking at a map to make sure you know where you have to go, and setting your alarm (and a back-up, if you tend to hit the snooze button a lot!). Having a stressful morning tends to start you on the wrong track for the day. Try to avoid the stress with some thoughtful planning the night before.

The second element of your time-management routine that can help you reduce your stress and put you in control of your schedule is a strategy called *back planning*. The basic idea of back planning is to look ahead to the deadline for a task, estimate the amount of time it will take to complete the task, and then establish a starting point for the task. For example, if you know that you need to write a 20-page paper for English composition and you expect that all of the research, writing, editing, formatting, and printing will take two weeks, then you can schedule time to start the project at least two weeks before its deadline.

Back planning works for short-term planning, too. If you know that your morning class starts at 8:30 A.M. and it typically takes 45 minutes for you to complete your entire morning routine and find parking, then you know that you need to walk out the door of your dorm or apartment no later than 7:45 A.M. to be on time. Establishing these short-term and long-term milestones will help you stay on track to meet deadlines and reduce the stress that's often associated with running behind.

LOOKING OUT FOR TIME-MANAGEMENT PITFALLS

Avoid the "Black Holes" of Technology and Procrastination

Often portrayed in science fiction movies or scientific documentaries, black holes in space absorb everything around them, including light. From the perspective of managing your time and energy, television, video games, and social media (such as Facebook and Twitter) have the potential to be virtual black holes in your life. You may plan on watching television for only 10 minutes, but chances are good that you'll still be sitting in front of the screen two hours later—and that you'll have accomplished nothing during that time. Playing video games has the capacity to be even more time consuming because of the interactive nature of today's games. Social media have emerged as yet another potential black hole, consuming both your time and attention by feeding continual distractions to you throughout the day.

As you establish strategies for managing your time and energy during your college experience, we urge extreme caution in your use of any of these items. All three are popular among college students, certainly, but if you don't use them in moderation, they will absorb your time and energy and leave little left over for your academic pursuits.

Indulging in media and technology are not the only ways to avoid doing your work in college. In fact, you'll most likely find a variety of ways to procrastinate. Cramming for quizzes and exams, pulling all-nighters to finish papers and projects, and missing work or skipping classes to finish assignments on time are all examples of procrastination. Any type of last-minute, hurried effort to meet a deadline tends to produce relatively poor academic performance and to cause a tremendous amount of emotional, physical, and social stress. However, using these desperate strategies is avoidable! With effective back planning, you can eliminate the need to stay up all night before an exam or to miss other classes to finish an assignment.

Image courtesy of Miami Dade College - North Campus

Professor Valarie De Angelis, M. Ed.

To avoid procrastination, the single biggest obstacle you need to overcome is putting off starting the project. Procrastination typically occurs when we (yes, professors sometimes procrastinate, too) are confused, intimidated, or overwhelmed by an assignment or task. Our fear gets the best of us, and we choose to forget about the assignment for a while, instead of trying to get started on it. Once we do get started, our fear tends to go away, and we discover that we're making more progress than we had expected.

In addition to risking running short of time, procrastinators face another problem: When the fear of missing the deadline and being late begins to creep in, they lose their ability to be clear thinkers and creative problem solvers. If you've ever been pressed to remember a phone number, locker combination, or other mental detail, you've probably discovered that it's more difficult to think clearly and solve problems when you're in a hurry. In the same way, it's difficult to be thoughtful and creative when you're trying to study for an exam or write a paper under time pressure.

We've spent a lot of time on procrastination, because it's such a common phenomenon in college and we see our students suffering unnecessary consequences from it. When you are assigned homework, projects, or papers, use back planning to clearly establish your start date for the project, as well as important milestones along the way (for example, "Read first two chapters by September 15"). Build those milestones into your calendar system, set time aside to do the work, and get started. If you establish the routine of regularly reviewing your calendar and to-do list and using back planning, you'll take control of your time and develop skills that will serve you well in college and throughout your life.

Multitask in Moderation

The ability to *multitask*—that is, to manage several activities or to pay attention to more than one task at a time—is often praised as an admirable and even necessary skill. In fact, many people believe that you can get more done and be more productive by multitasking than by doing one thing at a time. However, the scientific evidence doesn't support this common belief. In the article "Manage Your Energy, Not Your Time," Schwartz (2007, p. 67) explains:

> Many executives view multitasking as a necessity in the face of all the demands they juggle, but it actually undermines productivity. Distractions are costly: A temporary shift in attention from one task to another—stopping to answer an e-mail or take a phone call, for instance—increases the amount of time necessary to finish the primary task by as much as 25%, a phenomenon known as "switching time." It's far more efficient to fully focus for 90 to 120 minutes, take a true break, and then fully focus on the next activity.

If you tend to check your email, respond to text messages, monitor your Facebook status, and listen to your iPod while attempting to write a paper, study for an exam, or organize your calendar, you are undermining your ability to perform well, because performing these simultaneous tasks saps both your time and energy. Shut down the peripheral activities and stimuli and focus on the primary task at hand, and you'll find yourself accomplishing far more than you expected.

Manage Your Energy

Just as important as managing your time is managing your energy. Think about this scenario: You have the entire weekend off from work, and your spouse has taken the kids to visit their grandparents. That means you have 48 hours of complete solitude to write a research paper that's due on Monday. Sounds ideal, doesn't it? But what if you have the flu for those two days? And does having the time mean anything when you don't have the energy to do the work? What if you've just pulled two double shifts and haven't slept more than five hours in the past two days? Will you be able to use your free 48 hours productively, or will you need to take care of yourself?

INTEGRITY *Matters*

Do you tend to use your smartphone or another electronic device at the same time you're talking to someone in person? If so, you should know that this type of behavior may be considered rude and disrespectful by professors and college staff and is even an issue of personal integrity. Why? You're signaling to that person that he or she isn't important enough to warrant your full attention. One way to maintain integrity—and demonstrate respect—is to turn off your cell phone and put it in your backpack when you visit with a professor during office hours and when you attend class.

YOUR TURN

In approximately 250 words, describe how you feel when others haven't given you their undivided attention when you've wanted it.

Time is only valuable if you have the energy to use it well. Energy includes both physical and mental sharpness. We all experience variations in how sharp we feel throughout the day. Researchers sometimes refer to this as our *circadian rhythm*. The key is to understand yourself well enough to know when you are at the peak of your mental and physical alertness and when you are not.

In addition to falling and rising throughout the day, your energy level falls and rises throughout the week. Do you find yourself tired on Monday mornings but full of energy on Fridays? Or do you feel worn out by Thursday evenings but rejuvenated on Sundays? Depending on your work, school, and personal schedules, you'll find that you have regular bursts of energy at certain times of the week.

Once you've identified the hours in the day and the days in the week when you tend to be at your best, you can build your schedule to maximize your productivity during those times. You can also schedule activities that don't require as much effort or concentration during times when you aren't at your peak performance. Schedule activities such as writing papers, solving complex math problems, and reading assigned articles and books for peak times. It's also during these times that you'll most need your quiet, uncluttered workspace. Arranging your schedule and workspace will require some discipline and advanced planning, because you'll be tempted by other tasks and distractions. Most students are at or near the peak of their mental alertness shortly after waking up in the morning.

Image courtesy of Miami Dade College - North Campus

Professor Valarie De Angelis, M. Ed.

What should you do during those times when you aren't at your peak? First of all, recognize that it's OK to take breaks from working hard. In fact, it's actually more productive to take breaks than to try to work hard all day. The good news is that even when you don't feel mentally or physically sharp, you can still accomplish a lot. During those times, perform the common "time zappers" that can rob college students of their time: reviewing and sending emails, making phone calls, running errands, preparing meals, talking with roommates, taking a walk or swimming laps, or doing a form of meditative exercise.

Another way to help manage your energy is to become aware of what activities help you relax when you are stressed and what activities allow you to refill your energy reserves when you are dragging. If an activity rejuvenates you and helps you recharge, you may want to schedule it for times when you need to build up energy. If an activity helps you wind down, you may want to schedule it for after you have completed a major task.

CASE SCENARIOS

1. Janice has been doing very well in her classes. She has been able to manage her time wisely and adjust her schedule whenever something unexpected has come up. But this week promises to be hectic! Janet's boss expects her to stay late every day to finish a special project; she has an important exam on Thursday evening; her daughter has just come down with a stomach virus; and her husband will be out of town until late Friday. Janice's goal is to take care of each task without jeopardizing her job, her grade, or her daughter's welfare, but she knows that she can't realistically handle all these things. She decides to ask her professor if she can take the exam the following week, after finishing her boss's special project, and she asks a good friend to take care of her daughter so that she can work late every day until she finishes the project. At this point, Janice's top priority is her job.

   Use the following scale to rate the decision that has been made (1 = Poor Decision, 5 = Excellent Decision). Be prepared to explain your answer.

   Poor Decision   1   2   3   4   5   Excellent Decision

2. Glenn is a constant procrastinator. He feeds on the adrenaline that rushes through his body when he waits until the last minute to complete an assignment. However, the last time he did this, which was for his computer programming class, he ended up failing the assignment because he ran out of time. Then, he was exhausted for three days because he had stayed up for 36 hours straight. Glenn really wants to break his procrastination habit, so he's created a study group, in which he works together with classmates on assignments. For example, in his accounting class, each group member completes one of the homework questions, and then group members compile the answers to turn them in individually. Glenn has also decided to borrow a friend's paper from a history class to use as the foundation for his own paper, so that he doesn't have to spend so much time starting from scratch.

   Use the following scale to rate the decision that has been made (1 = Poor Decision, 5 = Excellent Decision). Be prepared to explain your answer.

   Poor Decision   1   2   3   4   5   Excellent Decision

3. Wanda was a good student in high school, taking Advanced Placement (AP) classes, making the honor roll, and being admitted to the National Honor Society. During her first four weeks of college, her classes have been easy, because they have covered material that she learned in her AP classes in high school. Looking ahead to next week, Wanda isn't worried that she has two tests and a paper due. The tests are in subjects she's familiar with, so she's planning to go over her lecture notes (she doesn't have many) the day before each test. The paper is due on Friday, so she's blocked off all of Thursday (after taking her second test) to complete it. Although she'll need to do research for the paper, she's confident that she can find what she needs searching the Internet on her laptop in her room.

   Use the following scale to rate the decision that has been made (1 = Poor Decision, 5 = Excellent Decision). Be prepared to explain your answer.

   Poor Decision   1   2   3   4   5   Excellent Decision

Take It with You

Action Item	Deadline	First Step
Create your priority list for this week.		
Commit to a time each day to review and update your priority list and calendar.		
Reduce the "black holes" in your schedule.		
Identify and participate in activities that give you energy.		

REFERENCES

Astin, A. (1997). *What matters in college*. San Francisco: Jossey-Bass.

Beck, M. (2012, June 19). Anxiety can bring out the best. *Wall Street Journal*, pp. D1–D2.

Nelson, D., & Low, G. (2010). *Emotional intelligence: Achieving academic and career excellence*. Boston: Prentice Hall.

PHOTO CREDIT

Alex Hinds/Shutterstock

7 Listening and Note Taking

Laura settled into her seat in the front row of her world civilization class. Class was about to start.

The professor began, explaining to students, "The clip we are about to watch discusses the ancient library in Timbuktu."

"I would much rather watch these videos than listen to Professor Reynolds talk," a classmate named Jamie whispered to Laura, causing her to miss the professor's explanation of the video.

"Hey? Do you have an extra pen?" Jamie asked, loud enough to be heard over the video. Laura handed Jamie a pen and made a note to fill in the gaps in her notes that resulted from being distracted.

After the video had ended, Laura's professor provided the information she had been waiting for. He said, "You have the material that was assigned for reading, the information I cover in the lecture, and then anything else that I bring in. All of this should be studied for the test."

"And he will put *everything* on the test," thought Laura.

Even with help from her mentor and the tutor in the learning assistance center, Laura had her work cut out for her. The book was arranged chronologically, but her professor lectured on causes and effects in history. Her notes seemed like a jumbled mess. Then, there were the tests that covered major themes, such as important reformers and federal policies. Laura struggled in this class to find the right note-taking method to accommodate all the different types of information.

As Laura headed out of class, her talkative classmate, Jamie, stopped her. He asked, "Do you want to share notes and study together? I don't have much written down, and I noticed you take good notes."

Laura didn't have much time to think about whether it would be helpful to study with someone who seemed so disorganized and inattentive, but she knew she would need help, too.

"Sure," she told Jamie before heading to her next class. "Bring your notes and book, and meet me in the library."

Like Laura, your success in college will depend in part on your ability to listen well and record what you've heard in class in your notes. To help you succeed in this effort, this chapter will help you do the following:

- Prepare for class.
- Practice active and critical listening.
- Effectively record and organize your in-class notes.

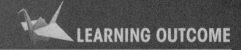

LEARNING OUTCOME

Create class notes using active listening techniques.

MyStudentSuccessLab (www.mystudentsuccesslab.com) is an online solution designed to help you 'Start strong, Finish stronger' by building skills for ongoing personal and professional development.

SUCCESS IN CLASS BEGINS WITH PREPARATION

Image courtesy of Miami Dade College - North Campus

In college, as in life, preparation is one of the keys to success. Much of your academic success will be determined by how well you prepare for your classes before they even begin. Just as you would invest time and effort to prepare for a first date, a job interview, or a meeting with a high-level executive, so you should prepare for a class before you walk into the classroom.

Because a great deal of information is typically shared during class, preparing effectively will be particularly important in helping you to listen well, to organize what you hear with effective notes, and to remember and recall the information later when you need it for projects and exams and your career. Here are a number of guidelines for ways to prepare effectively for class:

- *Read and study preassigned materials.* Your professor will often provide a syllabus that tells you what chapters or other written content is assigned for each day of class. If you take time to read the assigned materials before class, not only will you be more familiar with the content to be discussed in class, but you will also be able to learn more effectively and, in the long run, spend less time later preparing for quizzes and exams. Your professor might even provide a copy of the lecture notes in advance via the course website. If so, print out the notes and bring them to class. When you build your schedule for the term, include time for reading course materials before class. If you step into a class and have already read the assigned materials, you will better understand what the professor is talking about, you will be familiar with the terminology and concepts, and you will have good questions to ask in class for clarification and further learning. This will help you take notes more effectively and will enhance your class participation effectiveness, because you will be better equipped to actively participate in class discussions.

- *Minimize out-of-class distractions.* At times during your college experience, you may have to work late, stay up all night with a sick child, or help a friend who has just had a crisis. If not handled well, these stressful experiences might affect your performance in class. As much as possible, leave your personal life at the door and concentrate on the class that you are sitting in. How?

  - Put time into your schedule, outside class time, to address personal matters.
  - *Turn off* your cell phone while in class. Don't just set it to vibrate.
  - Build in 5 to 10 minutes before every class to clear your mind of personal issues and other distractions and to transition your mind to prepare for the class at hand. Reviewing the assigned readings or your notes from last class can aid in this process.

EXHIBIT 1

Tip	Explanation	Example
Prepare ahead of time.	Read all pages from textbooks, handouts, and extra material that your professor assigns or mentions.	Before the lecture on the American Dream in Arthur Miller's *Death of a Salesman,* read the entire play.
Minimize in-class distractions.	Make sure that you have few, if any, items or people near you that can get your attention.	Turn your phone to silent mode and stow it in your backpack before walking into class.
Maintain a positive attitude.	Stay positive about a class no matter what others have said negatively about it or what you have experienced so far.	On your way to class, think about five positive aspects of the class that will help you achieve your ultimate academic or career goal.
Minimize out-of-class distractions.	Your situation and thoughts can get in the way of concentrating on what is being said. Work to focus on the present, not the past or the future.	If there is something on your mind, write down your concerns before going to class and promise yourself to think about it after class is over.
Prepare physically.	Take care of yourself by getting enough rest and food or drink before you go to class. Wear appropriate clothing so that you will be comfortable.	Grab your jacket, an energy bar, and a bottle of water before you go to your classes.

- *Prepare for class psychologically by preparing physically.* Make sure you have eaten something before each class, so that you won't be distracted by a growling stomach. Moreover, dress in layers in case the room is an uncomfortable temperature. Nothing is more distracting than being too hot or too cold. Getting plenty of sleep the night before class will also help you pay attention and listen effectively. Although adequate sleep may be a luxury if you work a late shift or if you get up in the middle of the night to take care of a child, be sure you make an effort to get a good night's sleep as often as possible. You won't be able to maintain high concentration and retention or even good health without adequate rest.

Review Exhibit 1, which provides tips for preparing to listen.

ACTIVITY 1

Which of the following will be most challenging for you when you prepare for class: preparing physically, reducing out-of-class distractions, or completing assigned readings before class?

EFFECTIVE LISTENING IS BOTH ACTIVE AND CRITICAL

Active listening is a term that you may hear in college classes. Someone who listens actively is concentrating on what is being said and taking steps to remember the information. To be an active listener, you must decide that listening is a worthwhile activity and that important information is being shared.

Follow these tips to listen actively and effectively:

- Write down important facts, concepts, and terms in notebooks designated for specific courses.
- Use visual tools (charts, tables, arrows, numbers) to organize content in notes.
- Raise your hand and ask questions to clarify content or to resolve confusing concepts.
- Maintain an upright posture in the chair to keep your body in an alert position.
- Create acronyms and use other mnemonic devices to help organize and remember information.
- Write down questions, feelings, opinions, and other reactions in the margins of your notes for later review and consideration.
- Maintain a positive attitude about each class. Look for connections between content discussed in the class, your other classes, and your future career. Consider the possibility that at any moment, you could learn something new—something that you never knew before. That's an exciting prospect that can keep you engaged in the class, no matter what the topic or how it's being discussed.
- Avoid in-class distractions.

    1. Clear your desk of everything except your textbook, a pen, and paper. Stow other items in your backpack or underneath your desk or table.
    2. If you need to get anything out of your backpack during class (such as a dictionary), minimize the disruption by being as quiet as possible.
    3. If you find yourself next to a chatty classmate or one who likes to write notes to you, simply move. Even if you are politely listening to this person or reading his or her messages, you will be guilty of disrupting the class by association. Talkative classmates make it difficult for you and others to listen, and they distract you from taking good notes.

To Listen Critically Is to Listen Well

As stated earlier, active listening, much like active reading, involves focusing on the task at hand and concentrating on what's being conveyed. Another part of listening effectively is listening critically—or processing what you have heard and evaluating it. Listening critically will help you make decisions about what is important and what isn't

Meeting EXPECTATIONS

The college will expect that I ...	To meet that expectation, I will ...
Example: . . . minimize listening barriers when I'm in class.	Example: . . . I'll store my cell phone in my backpack to keep me from being distracted, and I'll sit at the front of the classroom.

important, what is objective and what is biased, and what should be stored for later and what should be discarded.

Listening critically is a skill that you should practice regularly. Your college professors will invite you to think critically and will challenge your assumptions at times. This may feel uncomfortable, but critical thinking is a key part of learning. As you get more comfortable with listening actively and critically, you'll move from merely listening and taking notes that reflect what your instructors have said to listening to evaluate and ask questions of the notes you have taken.

Here are some questions to consider as you work on listening critically:

It's in the SYLLABUS

By looking at your syllabus, determine how the information will be presented in a given course: Will it be presented by chapters, topics, or units? Also consider these questions:

- What are the note-taking expectations for the class?

- Is that information in the syllabus, or did you learn it from your professor or other students?

- *Speaker.* Is the speaker a credible source? How do I know? What possible biases does he or she have? What is his or her experience with the topic?
- *Message.* What is the speaker's purpose? What details does he or she use to convey the message?
- *Details.* Is the speaker using facts or opinions? How do I know? Which type of details work best for what the speaker is trying to convey?
- *Self-knowledge.* What do I already know about the topic? How does what the speaker is saying conflict or support my beliefs and opinions? Do I feel I have learned something new?
- *Larger picture.* How does what the speaker is saying fit into the larger picture? How can I relate his or her message to something I already know about life or the world at large? Are there any connections between what I have heard and what I have experienced?

Answering some of these questions will get you started on the right path to listening critically. Even though you will be listening critically and mentally asking questions of what you are hearing, you will still need to "tune in," rather than "tune out," when you hear something that you don't agree with or don't understand.

Remember, too, that *critical* does not mean *negative*. If you find that what you are hearing doesn't hold up to what you know about the subject or that the speaker isn't credible, ask questions that are respectful and curious. Most speakers don't mind being politely challenged or debated.

TAKING NOTES IS PART OF THE LISTENING PROCESS

There are numerous methods of taking notes for class. Your goal should be to find the note-taking strategy that works best for you.

Remember that you may have to adapt your note-taking style to each course, including each professor's teaching style, and to your own learning style preference. For example, outlining may work well in a history course in which the instructor writes key terms on the board and organizes the lecture around these key ideas. But if your professor prefers unstructured discussion, you'll need to adapt your note-taking strategy to make the most of disorganized information.

INTEGRITY *Matters*

There are websites where college students from across the country post their notes from various courses. It's tempting to download notes from these sites, rather than write your own. Some professors consider using other students' notes a form of plagiarism and a violation of their intellectual property rights. Also keep in mind the benefit of taking notes yourself: It helps you learn and remember the information better. If you simply copy someone else's notes, you won't get that benefit anymore.

YOUR TURN

In approximately 250 words, explain how you feel about using other students' notes from your classes instead of or in addition to your own.

Whatever you choose for the particular course, your learning style preference, and the specific situation, remember these tips when taking notes:

- *Listen for the main ideas.* Professors will slow down and emphasize details, terms, and definitions. They may even use verbal signposts, such as "The most important thing to remember is . . ." "This may appear on an exam," and "Two crucial points about . . ." If the instructor writes or hands out an outline, you can be sure that it contains the main points of the lecture.
- *Leave plenty of "white space" (blank areas on the paper) when taking notes.* Don't try to fill your page with as much information as possible. You will need the white space to add more notes or to connect ideas once you have reviewed them.
- *Review your notes as soon as possible after class.* Waiting for two weeks to review your notes will ensure that you won't remember everything that you have written or how it all fits together. Most experts suggest reviewing notes within two days of a class.

Knowing How Information Is Presented Can Improve Your Note Taking

Learning to listen effectively is the first step to taking good notes, but you'll also benefit from understanding how information can be presented during a lecture. As you attend more classes, you'll probably notice that professors have certain ways in which they present their materials. Some follow the text, presenting information in the same order. Others lecture only on new material that can't be found in the text or other course materials. Others use a combination of the two methods. Reading assigned chapters and other materials before class will allow you to determine which information in the lecture is new and which has been covered in the assigned reading materials.

Here are some of the different ways that course materials might be organized:

- *Chronological:* Details are arranged in time (first this happened, then this happened, etc.).

Example of Chronological Lecture Notes

1801: United Kingdom of Great Britain is created.

1803: Louisiana Purchase is made by Thomas Jefferson.

1815: Battle of Waterloo signals end of Napoleon's career.

- *Cause/Effect:* Details are arranged by presenting a cause and then its effects, or an effect and then its causes.

Example of Cause/Effect Lecture Notes

Cause: Civil War

Effects: slavery ended, industrialism began, nation brought back together, federal government proved stronger than states

- *Compare/Contrast:* Details are arranged by similarities and differences.

Example of Compare/Contrast Lecture Notes

Similarities between Robert Frost and Walt Whitman: they were males; they used nature in their poetry; and they were considered "poets of the people."

Differences between Frost and Whitman: Frost's poetry is more structured, while Whitman's is more open and loose; Whitman's speakers are more positive and upbeat than Frost's; Whitman lived during the 19th century, while Frost lived in both the 19th and 20th centuries.

- *Most important/Least important:* Details are arranged in order of importance. The most important detail can come first, with minor supporting details to follow, or the least important details can start a list, with a major detail to follow.

Example of Most Important/Least Important Lecture Notes

Truman Commission (1946)*

Barriers to equal opportunity & toward equalizing opportunity (most important sections in the doc.)

Number who should receive higher education & the role of education (2nd most import.)

The need for general education & a time of crisis (least import. secs.)

*first pres. comm. on hi. ed.

THE UNWRITTEN RULES

Of Listening and Note Taking

The ability to listen well is arguably more critical to your success than your ability to speak well. Why else would you have two ears but only one mouth?

By preparing for class, listening well, and taking good notes, you can actually reduce your study time. Professors will hesitate to suggest this, because they don't want students to reduce how much time they devote to studying. But the fact is that if you listen to, process, and organize information effectively the first time, you won't take as long to review and remember the same information the second time.

Sitting next to your friends or students you know in class might not be the best idea. The probability of being distracted increases when you are close to people you know. It might be socially awkward to tell friends that you're not going to sit next to them in class, but your academic performance will stand to gain from making wise choices.

Professor Lottie M. Tucker-McMillan, M.Ed.

Image courtesy of Miami Dade College - North Campus

Note-Taking Strategies: Pick What Works Best for You

Once you understand how each of your professors tends to present information or how the information is structured in your course materials, you can develop your own strategy for organizing your notes. Here are some strategies that you can try for yourself.

Outlining

Using an outline is a good method for taking notes if the instructor is organized and offers information in a logical pattern. Some instructors encourage outlining by writing key words and concepts on the board or an overhead projecting device. If your instructor organizes lectures or class discussions in this manner, you'll be able to write an outline for your notes quite easily. The key to making an outline effective is to provide plenty of space between items so you can fill in the blank spaces with extra information.

The T-System

Cornell University professor Walter Pauk (2004) developed a system for note taking that has been popular with many students. The *Cornell system,* also known as the *T-system,* is ideal for learners who benefit from the visual impact of organized notes, and it can benefit other types of learners, such as Laura, because it is an organized way to take and review notes.

The key to the Cornell system is to divide your notebook paper before you begin writing. To do so, draw a horizontal line across a piece of paper 2 inches from the bottom of the page. Then draw a vertical line from the horizontal line to the top of the page about 2 inches from the left-hand margin. The page should look like Exhibit 2.

The largest area, the right-hand column, is used for taking notes during a lecture. The left-hand column is used for writing down questions while taking notes in case there is material you don't understand or there are possible exam questions that you think about as you are writing. The final section, at the bottom, is reserved for summarizing your notes as you review them. The act of summarizing should help you understand and remember the information.

Adapting Your Notes for Different Disciplines

Learn how to adapt your note-taking format or style for different classes and subjects:

- *Art:* In an art appreciation class, you'll need to identify eras (twentieth century), movements (Cubism), and artists (Picasso), as well as their characteristics, as seen in drawings, paintings, and sculptures. Quickly sketching the works in your notes and listing the characteristic details will help you record the information you are

EXHIBIT 2

Add questions or important notes here.	Write notes here.

Add summary of notes here after you read through them.

receiving through lectures. You may also notice that in the study of art, there are times of intense change (usually coinciding with a world or cultural event), followed by periods in which artists imitate or slightly modify the new styles. As you review your notes, look for patterns within groups of artworks and for points of contrast.

- *Music:* In a music appreciation class, follow the same note-taking suggestions as for an art appreciation class. But instead of re-creating a painting or sculpture in your notes, write down descriptions of what you hear and what the sounds remind you of: Are the sounds fast or slow? Do you hear one instrument or many? Does it sound like a stampede or a trip down a lazy river? "Translating" music samples into written notes, as well as reviewing music clips on your own, will strengthen your understanding of the material. As with your art notes, when you review, look for patterns across movements and eras and identify contrasting ideas and elements.

- *Literature:* Taking notes in a literature class will require you to complete the assigned readings before class and to have annotated and highlighted your text. Because literature classes, even survey classes, focus more on discussion than on lecture, you'll want to be prepared to take notes on the analysis. As with music and art classes, being familiar with basic terminology before you get to class will help you take better notes. As you review your notes, look for ideas that pull the different readings together.

- *Languages:* Foreign language classes center more on speaking and interacting than on listening to lectures. Taking notes will not necessarily be advantageous, for you'll need to focus all your attention on listening actively, processing what you hear, and then interacting. Daily preparation is essential to learning a foreign language. Take notes as you encounter new material, and ask questions in class to clarify anything you don't understand. Be sure to review any notes that you do take soon after the class. As you review your notes, categorize content, such as "Irregular verbs," and include any tips for using or remembering the parts of speech.

- *Science:* Learning concepts and processes is key in science classes, and your notes should reflect that. Prepare for class by reading assigned materials, making note of new vocabulary words, and studying diagrams and figures in the textbook and handouts. As with any class, ask questions if you're having trouble following the steps of a process. As you review your notes, consider the different ways that you can represent these concepts and processes visually and physically to help you remember them better.

- *History:* History class lectures are usually presented in chronological order, so using the tips provided earlier for information that follows a time sequence will help you take notes in these classes. However, you will also be required to move beyond specific dates and events by considering overall themes, ideas, and movements. In addition to chronological order, cause/effect organization may be used in lectures, in which you list and elaborate on the effects of a cause or the causes of an effect. An example of a cause/effect lecture topic in a history class is "The economic and social effects of the end of the Civil War." As you review your notes, look for major themes and try to recall actions that led to important events.

Image courtesy of Miami Dade College - North Campus

- *Math:* Taking good notes in your math classes will require you to prepare for and attend each class meeting. As with studying a foreign language, studying for math should be an everyday occurrence, because the skills you learn in each class build on the skills you learned in the class before. When reviewing your notes, recopy them and make sure that you understand, line by line, each problem that you copy. If you have any questions, write them in the margins of your notes and ask questions during the next class meeting.

ACTIVITY 2 Complete the Following Table Based on the Courses You Are Taking This Semester

Course	Typical Presentation of Information by Instructor	Method for Taking Notes

By preparing in advance for class, listening both actively and critically, and taking effective notes, you can greatly enhance your college success.

CASE SCENARIOS

1. Juan is taking a visual arts class and having trouble making sense of his notes each week, because they contain information that pertains to specific works of art. The instructor doesn't hand out reproductions of the art, so students must sketch the pieces during class, which takes most of them a long time. Juan has difficulty sketching and writing quickly, so he decides that it would be best just to listen while the professor lectures. Juan plans to print out copies of the artworks from the Internet and make notes on the copies at home.

    Use the following scale to rate the decision that has been made (1 = Poor Decision, 5 = Excellent Decision). Be prepared to explain your answer.

    Poor Decision ← 1 ——— 2 ——— 3 ——— 4 ——— 5 → Excellent Decision

2. Theo borrowed Jon's notes for his College Algebra class and promised to return them before the next exam. Unfortunately, Theo has lost the notes, and with only two days left before the exam, he isn't sure what to do. Jon is a good student and probably doesn't need the notes as much as Theo does, but Theo wants to be able to borrow notes from Jon in the future. Theo decides to borrow another classmate's notes, copy them, and then give the copies to Jon after explaining what happened.

    Use the following scale to rate the decision that has been made (1 = Poor Decision, 5 = Excellent Decision). Be prepared to explain your answer.

    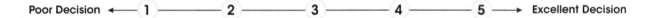

    Poor Decision ← 1 ——— 2 ——— 3 ——— 4 ——— 5 → Excellent Decision

3. Karla has a learning disability, and she struggles with taking notes. Her counselor has assigned her a note-taker. Now that Karla is getting help with writing down notes, she has stopped preparing for class and stopped listening closely. But sometimes, she doesn't get the notes from her note-taker until a week later. Instead of complaining to her counselor, Karla decides to ask another classmate if she can borrow his notes each week.

    Use the following scale to rate the decision that has been made (1 = Poor Decision, 5 = Excellent Decision). Be prepared to explain your answer.

    Poor Decision ← 1 ——— 2 ——— 3 ——— 4 ——— 5 → Excellent Decision

Take It with You

Action Item	Deadline	First Step
Develop a plan of action for preparing for each class.		
Develop an active listening plan, and gather the necessary notebooks and other supplies for doing so.		
Practice critical listening in every class.		
Practice different note-taking strategies to learn which ones work best in different situations.		

REFERENCE

Pauk, W., & Owens, J.R. (2004). *How to study in college*. Boston, MA: Cengage.

8 Studying and Test Taking

Image courtesy of Miami Dade College - North Campus

Studying the origins of life in Biology 101 was becoming an exercise in personal survival. Juanita, Evan, Michael, and Laura had formed a study group early in the semester, and it had become a precious lifeline.

"So much work for just one class!" Michael exclaimed. "It's insane!"

Juanita added, "I'm taking world literature and psychology. The reading alone takes me hours each night."

Michael thought he studied too much about the wrong things, and Juanita had severe test anxiety any time she took a test.

"Are you starting without me?" Laura asked as she dropped her heavy backpack on the booth seat by Michael.

"Of course not," Juanita said. "Michael was just complaining about how much work this class is."

"My mother finished her degree right before I started school, and I remember how much she studied. If she can do it, I think I can, too," Laura said.

"Does anyone know what the next test will cover?" Michael asked.

"I have to study everything, even if I don't think it will be on the test," said Juanita. "If I'm not overly prepared, I won't do well. I suggest we start going over everything that we've done since the first chapter."

Evan offered his advice: "If we only review our notes, we should be fine. When was the last time you failed a test? You have to get something for just taking it."

This didn't make sense to Laura, so she made a suggestion: "We all seem to have different approaches, so it sounds like we would be better off studying by ourselves."

Juanita, Evan, Michael, and Laura need to develop a plan for studying and taking tests, and so do you. To put you on the path to success, this chapter will help you do the following:

- Develop effective study habits.
- Practice various memory strategies for studying.
- Apply strategies for taking different types of tests.

LEARNING OUTCOME

Recommend strategies for studying for and taking a test.

MyStudentSuccessLab (www.mystudentsuccesslab.com) is an online solution designed to help you 'Start strong, Finish stronger' by building skills for ongoing personal and professional development.

STUDYING IS A NECESSARY LIFELONG HABIT

Professor Ginny Peterson-Tennant, Ph.D.

Image courtesy of Miami Dade College - North Campus

As mentioned in an earlier chapter, theThe book *What Matters in College* (Astin, 1993) provides strong evidence that the amount of time students spend practicing what they're trying to learn (called *time on task*) is *the* single greatest predictor of academic success.

With this in mind, the best advice for taking tests is plain and simple: Study for every test—no exceptions. By studying for every test in every class, you'll develop the habits needed for success in your studies, your career, and your life.

Here are some specific tips for developing effective study habits:

- *Set a time and a place for studying that work well for you.* Put regular, ongoing appointments on your calendar specifically for studying the content from each class you're taking. Begin these appointments the first week of the term.
- *Designate a specific location for studying.* Find a place that's quiet and comfortable and that has good lighting and enough space for your supplies and books. The best location may be away from your dorm, home, or apartment.
- *Make arrangements for your children (if applicable).* Make the most of children's nap and sleep times, or find a reliable babysitter. If you have classmates with similar child-care needs, consider babysitting swaps to give each of you time to study regularly.
- *Set goals for your studying.* Are you trying to memorize content, to understand how a process works, or to solve a math problem? Start each study session by identifying what you're trying to accomplish.
- *Study actively.* Instead of simply rereading notes or passively reviewing the major headings in your textbook, do activities such as the following:
  - Rewriting or summarizing your notes
  - Rearranging the order of materials—for instance, from most important to least important, from least important to most important, in chronological order, and so on

Meeting EXPECTATIONS

The college will expect that I . . .

Example: . . . *spend a considerable amount of time studying for tests.*

_____

_____

_____

To meet that expectation, I will . . .

Example: . . . *work with a study group to prepare for tests.*

_____

_____

_____

- Making connections between what you have learned in the chapter, unit, or class and what you have learned at other times and places
- Making connections between what you have learned in class and what you have experienced in the real world
- Explaining concepts to someone who is not familiar with the topic
- Making visual representations of materials

USING MEMORY STRATEGIES CAN HELP YOU REMEMBER AND LEARN MORE DEEPLY

Research on the human brain has shown that spending more time actively learning a subject can translate into deeper learning and that having a positive attitude toward a challenging learning situation will result in learning more. Why? As you spend more time studying and engaged in active learning with a positive attitude, you'll remember more of what you have learned, because you'll have moved information from your short-term memory to your long-term memory. Those are the two types of memory: short term and long term.

When you meet someone, you keep that person's name and face in your short-term memory. In general, you can store only five to nine items at a time in short-term memory. If you try to add more items, you'll find that some of them slip away (Miller, 1956). Test your short-term memory by completing Activity 1.

ACTIVITY 1 Short-Term Memory Test

Glance at the following chart of words for 30 seconds. Then cover up the list and write down the words you remember. You don't have to list the words in the same order that you've seen them.

cup	paper	pencil	magnet	ruler	scissors
spoon	towel	tape	apple	knife	straw

How well did you do? If you remembered five to nine items, then you can consider your short-term memory average. It takes some work, though, to transfer information from your short-term memory to your long-term memory.

Memorizing Is an Important Skill

Modern technologies—including computers, smart phones, and ebook readers—make it easy for us to have a lot of information at our fingertips. With information so accessible, we might think that we don't need to memorize anything anymore.

The truth is, however, that having effective memorization skills is very important to college success. Quizzes, exams, and other types of tests are often *closed book,* which means that you can't refer to your textbook, notes, or other materials during the test. And because most tests are timed, you don't have enough time anyway to search for information while trying to answer a question. You either know the answer or you don't. For these reasons, it's very important to develop effective memorization skills.

Mnemonic Devices Can Help You Remember

Mnemonic devices are memory aids or strategies that help you remember items, concepts, or series of events. Usually, mnemonic devices are *not* helpful for deep learning, but they are helpful for learning the detailed content that often lays a foundation for deep learning.

Image courtesy of Miami Dade College - North Campus

Professor Lottie M. Tucker-McMillan, M.Ed.

For example, during your college experience, you may need to name all the bones in the human body or all the amendments in the U.S. Constitution. At these times, you may find yourself using mnemonic devices as part of your learning process.

Device 1: The Roman Room

Return to the list of words in Activity 1, and think about how you can remember all the items. The ancient Romans are credited with being able to remember significant amounts of information by using a technique called the *Roman Room*, also known as the *Memory Palace* and *loci method* (Foer, 2007). This visualization technique can be useful when trying to remember a string of seemingly unrelated items or complex materials that need to be pulled together.

To create a Roman Room, visualize a familiar place, such as a room in your house. If the room is connected to other rooms, then you will have more "places" to put ideas. When you visualize your room, pay particular attention to the items that are already in the room, such as furniture or favorite pictures, and to the room's unique details, such as peeling paint. The more vivid the visualization, the better able you will be to remember the items you place in the room.

To see the Roman Room or loci method in action, complete Activity 2.

ACTIVITY 2   Roman Room

Take another look at the same chart of words:

cup	paper	pencil	magnet	ruler	scissors
spoon	towel	tape	apple	knife	straw

Now think about placing these items in your kitchen. Put the *straw* in the *cup* and place them both in the cabinet. *Tape* the *paper* on the front of the cabinet. Place the *towel* on the counter next to the *apple, spoon,* and *knife.* Then put the *pencil, ruler, magnet,* and *scissors* in the drawer.

Take 30 seconds to describe the kitchen, or describe your own Roman Room with the items listed. Then cover up both the list and the description of the room, and see how many items you can remember. Write the words on a separate piece of paper.

Did you remember more words this time? If not, then visualization may not be the only type of mnemonic device you need to help remember a lot of detailed information.

Device 2: Acronyms and Acrostic Sentences

Other mnemonic devices may benefit students with different learning style preferences. Acronyms and acrostic sentences are two methods that may help students with a verbal learning style preference.

To form an acrostic sentence, take the first letter of each item in a series to create a descriptive sentence that helps you remember the items and their order. For example, music students remember the order of the notes on the lines of the treble clef staff (E, G, B, D, F) with the sentence "Every Good Boy Does Fine." To recall the order of biological groupings used in taxonomy (Kingdom, Phylum, Class, Order, Family, Genus, Species), students remember "Kids Prefer Cheese Over Fried Green Spinach."

To create an acronym, take the first letter of each item in a series and form another word or string of characters. Acronyms that we use every day include AIDS (acquired immune deficiency syndrome), SADD (Students Against Drunk Driving), REM (rapid eye movement), and SCUBA (self-contained underwater breathing apparatus). Acronyms that many students have used to help remember terms and the orders of items include ROY G BIV (the colors in the rainbow: red, orange, yellow, green, blue, indigo, and violet) and FACE (the notes in the spaces of the treble clef staff).

The list you've worked with contains too many words to create an acronym, but you can create an acrostic sentence (or two) using the initial letter of each word. Do this by completing Activity 3.

ACTIVITY 3   **Acrostic Sentences**

Write one or two acrostic sentences using these letters:

C	P	P	M	R	S
S	T	T	A	K	S

The order of the items isn't important, so feel free to rearrange the letters to make your sentence(s).

Here's an example sentence using the letters in the first row:

Creative People Produce Many Real Skits.

Device 3: Rhymes and Songs

Rhymes and songs are another type of mnemonic device. Although they are a little more difficult to compose than acronyms and acrostics, they often appeal to auditory learners. Who doesn't remember sayings such as "Thirty days hath September . . ." (to name the days in the months) and "In 1492, Columbus sailed the ocean blue" (to recall the year that Columbus set out for the New World)?

Again, these memory strategies work best for learning simple information. It will take more work to remember the cultural and economic effects of Columbus's discovery of the New World, for example.

Device 4: Chunking

Ideally, you will take time to explore a variety of memory strategies, trying them out until you find the one that works best for the subject matter and your own learning style preference. But if you're like many students, you'll need a memory strategy to work quickly as you cram before a test.

Students who cram may be successful in remembering content when they take the test the following day, but they won't likely remember the content weeks, months, or years later. That's why professors and tutors discourage students from cramming. It may work some of the time, and it's better than not studying at all for a test. Regardless, cramming often produces additional anxiety and stress, and the material you learn will not likely be stored in your long-term memory when you need it later.

With this warning in mind, consider that at some time, despite your best intentions, you will need to learn key concepts in a short amount of time. To do so, you should learn a fail-safe memory technique.

One method, called *chunking*, is similar to the Roman Room or loci method in that items are grouped to allow the brain to make connections with them, making it easier to recall the information later. The goal in chunking is to reduce a large number of items to only five to nine items. To see chunking in action, try to memorize the following 10-digit number:

5114796210

You may find it easier to remember the number by chunking the digits the way a phone number is divided:

511-479-6210

You probably don't realize that you chunk any time you memorize a phone number or account number (such as your bank account or Social Security number). In each case, you take a series of seemingly random numbers and put them together in groups.

To practice this mnemonic technique, do Activity 4, in which you memorize a variety of memory-related terms.

ACTIVITY 4   Chunking

Use the following list of key terms:

acrostic	mnemonic device
acronym	rhyme
chunking	Roman Room
cramming	short-term memory
loci method	teaching others
long-term memory	

First, make sure that you know the definition of each term. Record the definition next to each term:

acrostic _____

acronym _____

chunking _____

cramming _____

loci method _____

long-term memory _____

mnemonic device _____

rhyme _____

Roman Room _____

short-term memory _____

teaching others _____

Next, group the items logically. Then, complete the chunking with the remaining terms. For example, here's one way to group some of the terms:

Mnemonic devices are strategies for remembering items, and they include **acrostics, acronyms, rhymes,** and **Roman Rooms.**

How else could the terms be chunked? Use a separate sheet of paper to group them in various ways.

DIFFERENT TESTS AND TEST QUESTIONS REQUIRE USING DIFFERENT STRATEGIES

Although the terms *test* and *exam* are often used interchangeably, they have slightly different meanings. A *test* is a set of questions or problems that are used to evaluate one's skills, aptitudes, and abilities on a certain topic. Usually, a test assesses students'

THE UNWRITTEN RULES
Of Studying and Taking Tests

- **Cramming for a test or pulling an all-nighter is rarely useful.** If you try to study for a test just a day or a few hours in advance, you won't remember much of what you study. Also, the stress caused by your procrastination will probably deplete your ability to think creatively and critically.

- **Credit is credit, even if it's partial credit.** Suppose you have to answer an essay question that's worth 20 points, and you're confident that you know part of the answer but not all of it. Take the time to do well on the part that you know so you will get some credit for the answer.

- **Prepare yourself for the test conditions as much as the test itself.** Depending on your university's schedule, each of your final exams may take as long as three hours. When's the last time that you actually sat in one place for three hours working on a test or exam? You wouldn't think of preparing for a marathon by running 100-yard sprints, so don't prepare for a three-hour exam by practicing in 20- or 30-minute

sessions. The only way to perform well during a lengthy exam is to prepare yourself for thinking and writing for that block of time.

- **After the professor hands out the exam, if you don't understand a question, ask privately for clarification.** It will be up to the professor to decide how much help and clarification to provide, but it never hurts to ask. Don't start writing your answer until you completely understand the question.

- **Really long answers are rarely really good answers.** When faced with an essay question about a broad topic, students are tempted to write everything they know about it in the hope that something they write will satisfy the professor. This is the "everything but the kitchen sink" essay answer. This type of answer is rarely effective. To write a good essay response, pay attention to the verb or verbs used in the question. Being asked to *compare* is different from being asked to *evaluate.* Then write an answer that directly answers the question in a complete but concise manner.

knowledge and skills related to part of a course. An *exam,* however, is by definition an assessment of the content of an entire course or program. *Final exams* are sometimes called *comprehensive* or *cumulative exams,* because they cover what students have studied all semester or term.

Unless your professor tells you directly what will be on a test, assume that anything he or she assigned or covered in class may be included. Just about every college student has a story about taking a test that covered only the reading assignments and not what was discussed in class. These students were surprised to realize that studying their lecture notes wasn't enough to do well on the test.

The following is a list of materials that you may be "fair game" for a test in any class:

- Materials from lectures, discussion, and in- and out-of-class activities
- Information provided by guest speakers
- Information from workshops or field trips
- Information from multimedia productions, such as videos and audios
- Content from assigned readings, including chapter in the text and other publications
- Materials from handouts, including PowerPoint slides and outlines

You can also be assured of encountering a variety of types of tests and test questions. Take clues from what you do in class to help determine what kinds of tests and questions you may come across. For example, if your professor spends time applying information from a chapter during class or has you do this as an assignment, then he or she will likely prepare test questions that ask you to apply the information, as well. Listen for clues that professors give, such as "You should write this down" and "This is a really important point." Other cue phrases include "You may see this again on a test" and "If you saw this problem on a test, how would you answer it?" When you

It's in the SYLLABUS

Look at each class syllabus for clues about the tests you will have. Consider these questions:

- What types of test questions do you anticipate?

- What evidence in the syllabus leads you to believe you will have certain types of test questions? (*Hint:* Look at the course description, if included.)

- How often will you have tests?

hear these phrases, write them down and review them when studying your other notes. A professor who says these things is begging you to take note!

Test Questions Will Vary, and So Should Your Answers

There are two general categories of question types: objective and subjective. *Objective* questions usually require lower-level thinking. They ask you to recall facts and concepts, usually in the forms of multiple-choice, true/false, fill-in-the-blank, and short-answer questions. *Subjective* questions ask for your opinions about the content or ask you to apply the content in new ways. Essay and problem-solving (critical-thinking) questions are considered subjective, because they can be answered correctly in a variety of ways.

Sometimes, objective questions are easier to answer because the correct answer is included among the set of choices that's provided. However, answering objective questions can demand significant brainpower, especially when you must provide an answer for a question that gives very few clues, which is often the case with fill-in-the-blank questions. Since objective questions usually have single correct answers, some students believe that subjective questions have no wrong answers. While that may be somewhat true, there are effective ways to answer subjective questions. The following sections discuss typical types of test questions and how to answer them.

Multiple Choice

When answering a multiple-choice question, the first step is to read the question or statement carefully. Mark any special words in the question or statement that are keys to its meaning, such as *not, always,* and *only.*

Next, read each answer choice carefully, and eliminate any that are obviously wrong. If you have to guess, eliminate any answer with a misspelled or incorrect term (usually a sign that the instructor has hurriedly added false answers) and any answer that's shorter than the others. Also pay attention to choices such as "All of the above" and "None of the above." If you can determine that at least two of the choices are correct, then "All of the above" is probably the correct answer. Likewise, if at least two of the choices are incorrect, then "None of the above" is probably the correct answer.

When studying for a test that will include multiple-choice questions, be sure you know all the materials well. Also practice answering multiple-choice questions by using those in your textbook (or on a companion textbook website, if one is available) or creating your own multiple-choice questions based on the materials you are studying. Work through the questions alone, or share and practice with a classmate who has also created multiple-choice questions.

Matching

The matching section on a test usually presents two columns of information: a list of words or phrases and a list of descriptors. Your goal is to match corresponding items from the two columns—a term with its definition, for instance.

Professors who use matching sections usually require the basic recall of information, but you should read the directions carefully. There may be more than one match for an item in the list, or there may be extra descriptors that do not match anything. These *distractors* are included to make sure you know the content well enough to make the right decisions.

To complete a matching section, first read through both lists of information. Try to determine if there might be multiple matches or extra descriptors. In recording your answers, make sure that you write down the correct letter to match each word or phrase in the list. If you don't know some of the answers, use the process of elimination to narrow down the possible choices by first matching the terms you know for sure. Also, when the terms are of different types (for instance, some are people, some are places, some are dates), you may be able to eliminate certain descriptors because they don't logically match up.

To study for matching questions, you will need to know major terms, people, and events from the class materials. Also keep in mind that professors often use definitions and descriptions that are similar to the ones in the text or glossary, rather than the ones directly from this kind of source, to test your understanding of the content. It may be helpful to rewrite your definitions and descriptions in your own words. If you have a study partner or group, ask them to do the same and share the answers they record.

True/False

True/false questions can be tough, even though they have only two possible answers: true or false. Guessing or randomly answering true/false questions should be done as a last resort. A better approach is to read each statement carefully, noting key words and phrases that could point to the correct answer, such as *frequently, sometimes,* and *a few.* These words and phrases usually indicate a true statement. Words such as *never, only,* and *always* usually indicate a false statement.

If you're struggling with a particular true/false statement, take a moment to "flip" the statement and see if your answer would switch from true to false or false to true. Using this strategy can help you work through double negatives and other confusing language.

To study for true/false test questions, use the study tips provided earlier for multiple-choice and matching questions. Your goal is to know the course material or content well enough that when you're presented with questions about it, you can recognize major concepts and questions. Also try writing out sample true/false questions that you think would make good additions to the test. Share them with a study partner or group, and take turns answering each other's sample questions.

Fill-in-the-Blank/Short Answer

Fill-in-the-blank and short-answer questions require you to recall specific information, such as definitions of key terms or items in a series. To complete these types of questions, first read the sentence or question carefully. Often, you will lose points for the question if you don't answer it exactly or misspell the correct term.

Fill-in-the-blank and short-answer questions can be particularly difficult if you aren't familiar enough with the materials. A good way to study for these questions is to create and use flash cards, which have a term or major concept on one side and a definition or description of the term or concept on the other side.

Problem Solving

Instructors use problem-solving, or critical-thinking, questions to have students demonstrate or apply the concepts or ideas they have learned. To answer a problem-solving question, first read the question carefully. Mark multiple steps or parts to the directions. Next, determine what information you'll need to solve the problem. Then, break

INTEGRITY *Matters*

Nearly 75% of college students admit to cheating at least once, as reported by Plagiarism.org (2012) and other sources. The reasons students give for cheating are many: Some don't believe that their professors notice or care about their work, while others believe that getting good grades is the most important goal, given the high standards demanded by scholarships and program admissions (such as nursing schools). Colleges do take cheating seriously, however, and often have no tolerance for students who cheat. Penalties can range from getting an F in the course to being expelled.

YOUR TURN

In approximately 250 words, describe why you think such a high percentage of college students have reported cheating. Also describe what colleges can do to help maintain an environment of academic integrity.

the problem into parts, and write down what process or operation you will need to perform. Work through the problem, and after you arrive at an answer, check the directions again to make sure you have adequately answered it.

Studying for a problem-solving test, such as a math or science test, will most likely involve practicing similar types of problems. Work through the additional problems in your textbook, homework assignments, and notes for extra practice. You may also find sample problems online, with answers provided so that you can check yourself.

Essay Questions

Instructors use essay questions to measure students' ability to analyze, synthesize, and evaluate the concepts they have learned. Essay questions evaluate much more than students' recall of facts or terms. You can be assured that you'll encounter many essay questions in college, because they allow students to demonstrate a deeper understanding of the materials.

In an exam context, the term *essay* can also refer to a question requiring a detailed, well-developed answer that uses material from the course to support a particular thesis or to describe a particular concept. Your answers to essay questions should not be based on your own opinions (unless the professor specifically asks for your opinions). Instead, your answers should demonstrate your understanding and recall of important information from the class (such as textbook readings and lecture notes) to address particular challenges or to explain certain ideas. Another important thing to remember about essay questions is that although you won't have a lot of time to answer them, your professor will still expect your responses to be thorough and clear.

To answer an essay question, always begin by reading the directions carefully. If the question has more than one part, be sure to mark each part and then answer it in the body of the essay. If the directions specify a length requirement (a number of words), be sure to meet or exceed it. And before you begin writing, create a brief outline of what you will cover in the essay.

Study for essay questions just as you would problem-solving questions by practicing. If your professor provides a list of topics or sample questions, use them to create outlines and then memorize the outlines. They will serve as the bases for your essays. If you don't receive sample topics or questions, then create your own by reviewing the course materials and your notes to identify topics that were emphasized in class or that you spent the most time on. These may be clues to possible essay questions.

CASE SCENARIOS

1. Sylvia's accounting professor announced to the class that he allows students to study from old tests. In fact, he provides a folder of previously used tests in the library for students to review. One of Sylvia's classmates, Maria, asked her if she wanted to study for the test, and she agreed. When the two met, Maria pulled out a copy of a test with the current semester's date on it. Sylvia questioned her, and Maria said that the professor gave her a rough draft of a test he decided not to use. When Sylvia went to class and took the test, she recognized every question, because the test was the same one that Maria had shown her. Sylvia decided to take the test without saying anything to her professor.

    Use the following scale to rate the decision that has been made (1 = Poor Decision, 5 = Excellent Decision). Be prepared to explain your answer.

    Poor Decision ← 1 — 2 — 3 — 4 — 5 → Excellent Decision

2. Ryan glided through high school without cracking open a book, but now that he's in college, he's realized that he doesn't know how to study very well. He's taking five classes: Intermediate Algebra, Reading Improvement, Introduction to Sociology, Speech Communication, and Concepts of Health and Wellness. Although it's early in the semester, he's already struggling through his health and math classes and has made low C's and a D on recent tests. Eager to do better, Ryan has asked some classmates to get together over beer and pizza to study for the rest of the semester.

    Use the following scale to rate the decision that has been made (1 = Poor Decision, 5 = Excellent Decision). Be prepared to explain your answer.

    Poor Decision ← 1 — 2 — 3 — 4 — 5 → Excellent Decision

3. Betty gets sweaty palms and feels like throwing up each time she has to take a test. She has actually failed and dropped classes because she couldn't calm down enough to take major tests. This semester, though, Betty wants to do better. She can't keep dropping and failing classes! Betty has talked to her classmates about what they do to ease test anxiety. One told her about an herbal tea drink that calms your nerves but makes make you very sleepy a few hours later. Another friend suggested taking an energy supplement to pep her up and keep her from worrying. Betty has decided to drink the tea before taking her test.

    Use the following scale to rate the decision that has been made (1 = Poor Decision, 5 = Excellent Decision). Be prepared to explain your answer.

    Poor Decision ← 1 — 2 — 3 — 4 — 5 → Excellent Decision

Take It with You

Action Item	Deadline	First Step
Schedule blocks of time on your calendar system for studying.		
Identify a specific location for studying.		
Complete practice tests.		

REFERENCES

Astin, A.W. (1993). *What matters in college.* San Francisco: Jossey-Bass.

Foer, J. (2007). Remember this. *National Geographic* 212(5), 32–55.

Miller, G. (1956). The magical number seven, plus or minus two: Some limits on our capacity for processing information. Retrieved from http://www.musanim.com/miller1956

Plagiarism.org. (2012). Did you know? Retrieved from http://www.plagiarism.org/plag_article_did_you_know.html

PHOTO CREDIT

Frederick Bass/Getty Images

9 Career Exploration

EVAN AND MICHAEL'S STORY

Image courtesy of Miami Dade College - North Campus

A big, red arrow pointed to the ballroom. In it, dozens of booths invited students to leave their resumes and to learn more about a variety of local and national businesses and industries.

Fresh from class, in jeans and his old university sweatshirt, Evan stopped to pick up a company brochure.

"I'm planning on going to all the booths," he told Michael. "Are you?"

Michael, wearing khakis and a white shirt, had done a little research and had already decided on the two booths he wanted to visit.

"No," he said. "I plan on finding the two companies I checked out on the Internet last night, telling them what I know about the open positions, and leaving my resume."

"Aren't you afraid you'll be cutting yourself short? Shouldn't you hit every one of the booths, just in case?" Evan asked.

"I don't know," Michael replied. "I guess with all my time in the military, I have a lot of experience doing different jobs."

"But there are so many options," Evan continued.

"Well, what degree can you earn that will get you a job that pays well?" asked Michael.

"I'm not sure," Evan told him.

"You won't be landing any jobs like that the way you are dressed today!" Michael said, smiling at his friend.

Evan pulled out 30 copies of his resume from his backpack and walked to the first table and introduced himself.

"Hi, I'm Evan," he said to a woman representing an aeronautics firm. "It's a pleasure to meet you. So, tell me what your company does and what I would do if I worked for you."

Michael walked straight to one of the two health care companies at the fair to deliver his resume.

Like Evan and Michael, you will have the opportunity to pursue a full-time career after you graduate from college—a career that capitalizes on your talents and abilities. To prepare you for a successful career, this chapter will help you to do the following:

- Identify careers that relate to your interests.
- Develop strategies for exploring a career.
- Establish a plan for networking to enhance career exploration and growth.
- Write an effective resume.

LEARNING OUTCOME

Create a career exploration plan.

MyStudentSuccessLab (www.mystudentsuccesslab.com) is an online solution designed to help you 'Start strong, Finish stronger' by building skills for ongoing personal and professional development.

YOUR CAREER STARTS HERE

It's in the SYLLABUS

Your course syllabi may help you in your career exploration. Look at what you are covering during the semester in each class. Also consider these questions:

- Do any topics really interest you?
- Do you find yourself drawn to certain subjects? What are they?
- Which professors will be helpful to you in the future?

Whether you know exactly what career you want or are still exploring the possibilities, your college experience can help you focus on what you want out of your professional life. Although it may seem like your career won't start until you're done with college, the exciting reality is that the decisions you are making today are already starting to form your career.

College is the time for exploring and preparing for a career, and the first step is to know your goals and what values you want to uphold.

Career Values and Goals Set the Course for Your Journey

Before you begin delving into the resources and services available at your college, take some time to reflect on what your career values and goals are. *Values* are personal and professional qualities and principles that are deeply important to you. For example, you may have a passionate interest in working for a company that makes products or provides services that have a positive impact on society or the environment. Or it may be critically important for you to work for an organization that is honest and ethical.

In addition to considering your values as they relate to your career, you may also want to consider what your goals are. *Goals* are tangible outcomes that you want to achieve in your personal and professional lives. Perhaps one of your goals is to move up quickly in a company, to find a business that will allow you to indulge in one of your values, or to travel and meet a diverse group of people.

When you get to the point that you'll be creating clear, realistic, and reachable career goals, your values will inform what you write down or tell others. Your values and goals will also help you talk with a career counselor, search for employment, and interview for a job.

Different Careers Mean Different Experiences

In addition to your personal values and goals, consider what you value in a career and what kinds of experiences you want to have. For example, do you value working with others in projects with strict deadlines, or would you prefer to work alone with little supervision? Your answer to this question and others can help you determine what you value and what careers may work best for you. If, for instance, you have a strong interest in writing but you prefer working with others, you may decide to choose a career that has many opportunities for collaboration when writing.

If you aren't sure where to start when considering your career values and goals, then check out various career assessment programs, such as DISCOVER and Kuder, at your career counseling center. There are also a number of books, such as Bolles's (2011) *What Color Is Your Parachute?* and websites that offer guidance for identifying your career interests, even at the early stages of your college career.

The career landscape can seem daunting and complex, especially because technology seems to cause careers to change quickly. Careers that existed 10 years ago may not exist four years from now, and careers that didn't exist a few years ago are

Meeting EXPECTATIONS

The college will expect that I . . .	To meet that expectation, I will . . .
Example: . . . *know what career I want to pursue when I graduate.*	Example: . . . *explore my options and take a proactive role to determine which careers would be best for me.*

now emerging. For this reason, don't put pressure on yourself to identify a specific company and job title for your career goal. Instead, keep your focus on the kind of career you want in terms of its general characteristics: work environment, type of industry, technical requirements, individual versus team environment, highly structured versus unstructured organizational structure and job functions, and so forth. Take time to browse career listings on websites (such as career-builder.com), and save copies of the posts that capture your interest. Doing these things will help you paint a picture that captures both your values and goals as they emerge and develop over time.

It's OK if your interests change over time. That will happen as you take more classes and gain new perspectives from your college experience. In fact, in today's work environment, the average individual will have several careers over his or her lifetime. What you're developing in college is the ability to identify your interests and abilities and to match them with the career opportunities in the marketplace. You may not want to face this reality now, but you may very well find yourself back in college later in life to pursue an advanced degree or certificate or a second bachelor's degree as you re-create yourself throughout your lifetime. As you learn to use the tools and resources discussed in the next section, you'll be encouraged to know that they can serve you well throughout your career journey.

Professor Lottie M. Tucker-McMillan, M.Ed.

THERE ARE SEVERAL WAYS TO EXPLORE YOUR CAREER

Chances are, several resources and events are available on your campus to support your efforts to explore and pursue your career options and opportunities. These include career counselors and professors, career fairs, and internships.

Image courtesy of Miami Dade College - North Campus

Career Counselors Can Be Your Best Supporters

Even though you won't pursue a full-time career until you graduate, commit yourself to meeting with a counselor your freshman year so you can put an effective plan in place for both internships and your career. Each college offers different services in its career center, but most provide access to interest inventories and resources on different careers, which can help you pinpoint which careers you are best suited for. In addition, career centers may offer help with writing a cover letter and resume and tips for interviewing for a job. Evan should spend some time in his college's career library to learn more about careers before he hits all of the employers at the career fair.

Don't forget that your professors can also be great career counselors. They often have connections with people in the field or have friends or relatives working in different industries. You never know when your sociology professor may have a contact at an accounting firm or your biology professor may have a connection with the human resources department at an advertising firm. Tell professors what you want to do as a career whenever you have a chance. They may be likely to remember you and your goals when they meet someone in your field of study.

Internships Give You and Your Employer a Chance for a "Test Drive"

Another work option for college students is an internship. An *internship* is a supervised position that allows a student to work for an organization before he or she graduates. Some internships are unpaid, which makes them less attractive to students who need to work. However, you may be able to earn academic credit for a paid or unpaid internship, so check with your advisor about this possibility well in advance.

Being an intern is a great way to make progress toward your degree and to explore a career at the same time. Another idea is to volunteer once or twice a week at a place of business. If you have a few extra hours a week or can trade college credit for an internship, then you should investigate the benefits of interning.

Why are internships such good opportunities for college students? One reason is that they allow you to work closely in a field that you may be interested in. In addition, being an intern can help you explore different ways that your major can be used in the workforce. For example, an English or journalism major may want to participate in an internship as a copywriter at a newspaper or as a technical editor at a publisher. A computer science major may want to intern at a small business to get practical experience with computer networking issues on a small scale. Opportunities like these can give you firsthand experience with using what you're learning in your degree.

Being an intern also allows you to network with others who can help you find a job once you graduate. Even if you decide that you don't want to work in the same area as your internship, you will have made contacts that may help you find a job in another field.

If you decide to intern, treat it as you would a job in your chosen career. Some employers rely on interns to complete certain projects each year, and they expect interns to be serious about the position, even if they don't get paid. Keeping a good attitude and being self-motivated are excellent ways to shine during your internship. In addition, be sure to meet regularly with your supervisor to ask questions and to get guidance on projects. Most of all, make the best of your unique opportunity, and add that experience to your resume.

NETWORKING OPENS DOORS FOR YOUR CAREER

Networking is defined as the "sharing of knowledge and contacts; getting the help you need when you need it from those from whom you need it . . . ; [and] building relationships before you need them" (Darling, 2010, p. 16). Now more than ever, networking is an essential part of an effective career search. If you ask 10 recent college graduates who have full-time careers how they landed their jobs, chances are that at least six of them will tell a story about how someone they knew helped them meet someone in the organization to get a first interview. If you establish good relationships with a variety of individuals across multiple companies and industries throughout your college experience—including your freshman year—then these individuals will become your primary gateway to getting initial interviews.

It's important to establish what networking can and cannot do for your career search. Effective networking throughout your college years can help you get your foot in the door at various organizations, and it may help you land that first interview. At that point, however, it's all up to you. Someone else's referral on your behalf is often enough for a recruiter to take time to give you an interview, but it's not enough for a recruiter to hire you. You have to prove yourself in the interview process, and after you've been hired, you have to prove yourself on the job.

In a competitive job market, in which hundreds of people are applying for a single position, landing that first interview is a crucial step. Networking can help you get there.

Networking Is More than Exchanging Business Cards

When you see the word *networking,* what scene or activity comes to mind? The stereotypical perception of networking is a bunch of people introducing themselves to each other and making small talk at a social or business function. Some people think they've

THE UNWRITTEN RULES

Of Career Planning

"The early bird gets the worm." Maybe you haven't heard this phrase before. It means that someone who is first to pursue an opportunity has a better chance of seizing it. This holds true for your career pursuit, as well. If you are proactive and ahead of your peers in developing a resume, building a network, and applying for internships, then you'll give yourself a better chance of securing a good job, both while you're in college and after graduating.

The best careers come from where you least expect them. While serving as a restaurant server or hostess, you might serve a client who turns out to be a major employer, recruiter, or entrepreneur. By demonstrating some interest in that person and listening well, you might pick up clues that open the door for you to introduce yourself and express interest in the company. Be ready to give your 30-second "elevator pitch" at any time—even in the bathroom!

Students can have business cards, too. If you have access to a computer, then you have what you need to design and print a professional-looking business card. Include your name, the university you attend, your major, and your contact information. Be sure to have some of these cards with you at all times.

E-portfolios are coming. An e-portfolio is a website where students compile carefully selected samples of their academic work and accomplishments to show to prospective employers and graduate schools. Increasingly, employers want to see more than just your resume. They want to see samples of your actual work, including papers you've written, computer programs you've developed, projects you've completed, and problems you've solved. If you start collecting and organizing your work immediately during your first term of college, then you'll have a lot more content to use for an e-portfolio when you're ready to build it.

done a good job of networking if they came home from an event with a lot of business cards in their pockets.

Networking is a lot more than that. It certainly begins with an initial point of contact, and for that, you need to make a professional first impression. How you dress, what you say, and how you act during the initial social exchange will be important. But once you've made that initial contact with someone, how you follow up and maintain contact with him or her really determines the value of your network.

Suppose that you're at a relative's wedding, and you meet someone who has a highly successful career at an accounting firm. At the time, you have no interest in accounting, nor do you know much about the company the individual works for. Even so, you take time to ask questions about the individual's career and organization, and you politely ask for his business card or contact information.

Was that networking? Yes, but you were just getting started! It's what happens after the introduction that matters most.

When you get home, you need to add that person's contact information to a database and then compose a follow-up email or personal letter. In it, express that you enjoyed meeting the individual and learning about his career, and say that you'd like to stay in touch as your college career progresses. If you have prepared a current resume, send it to the individual, even if you don't have a present interest in a career at his organization.

In the months and years to follow, use a calendar system to remind yourself to touch base with this person. Update him on your accomplishments in college, ask him about his career accomplishments, ask him questions about how he chose his career, arrange an informational interview at his firm, and share any news articles that you read that have something to do with his industry or company.

As you invest in this relationship over time, you'll build a connection that is far more extensive than what you had when you first met this person. Then, when you really need this individual and the others in your network to help you secure that first interview, they will know you well enough to trust in your personal qualities and professionalism.

When someone takes the risk of recommending you to a friend or associate for a job interview, that person is putting his or her own reputation at risk on your behalf. Asking for a recommendation is a significant request! Successful networking, over time, will establish a range of personal and professional relationships that can help you make the right connection at the right time when your career search gets into full swing.

If you wait until late in your college career to start networking, it will be far more difficult for you to prove your sincerity and professionalism through the test of time. Start networking early and build a broad network, because you never know where your interests may take you in the future.

Networking Face to Face

The most effective method of networking is to build relationships through face-to-face interactions. You can pursue a number of specific activities to help you form broad, long-term connections:

- *Join clubs on campus that suit your interests.* Even if a club is not career related, such as a drama club, you will meet people who may be future contacts for jobs.

Image courtesy of Miami Dade College - North Campus

- *Scan your school newspaper and announcements for events, such as guest speakers and discussion panels.* Colleges often bring in influential experts and industry leaders for speaking engagements. Attend these events when you can, not only to learn new perspectives but also to try to meet these individuals and introduce yourself.
- *Join a college ambassador club or another host-related student organization.* Many colleges have a student ambassador group that plays a lead role in hosting distinguished college guests, provides campus tours for visitors, and represents the college at community events, such as chamber of commerce meetings and special task forces and committees.
- *Consider a student leadership position on your campus.* Student leaders, such as members of the student council, often have special access to college administrators and community leaders.
- *Get involved in community service and philanthropic activities.* Industry and community leaders—the kinds of people who are ideal for including in your personal network—are often actively engaged in nonprofit organizations, community service activities, and philanthropy. You probably won't bump into the chief executive officer (CEO) of a large company in your daily life as a college student, but if you invest in community service and philanthropy, you might find yourself working next to someone who could eventually become a valuable member of your network.

As you pursue networking opportunities, carry them out with a genuine interest in making a contribution to the organization; don't participate just to meet people. Before you commit to any club, organization, community event, or philanthropic cause, be sure that it's something you believe in and are willing to support. Otherwise, your lack of sincerity and commitment will affect your reputation, and you'll do more harm than good. However, if you get involved in something that you feel committed to, the personal network of relationships you establish will open doors in your career that you never could have imagined for yourself.

Networking Online

One of the largest trends in networking is using social networking websites, such as LinkedIn and Facebook, to create networks of friends, family, and special interest groups. The possibilities seem endless for ways to use the Internet to connect with others who have special interests and activities or problems to solve.

With that said, if you decide to join a network that focuses on an interest of yours, such as computer programming, be sure to investigate who runs the group, what kinds of information are shared, and how active the group is. Some networks will be more active than others, which will make it easier to connect with others and get involved. Other networks or groups may be less active, which won't help you if you are trying to get to know others as potential contacts in the future.

Because creating networks of your own is so easy, you may want to consider creating an interest group if you can't find one related to your career of interest. Networking sites such as Facebook allow you to set up groups that can be used for professional, educational, or social purposes.

If you decide to set up a profile on a social networking site such as LinkedIn, take time to establish a profile that is well written, professional, and informative. These sites often allow you to post a photo, so provide one that shows you dressed professionally, as you would appear for a job interview. Upload your entire resume or the content of the resume, and make sure that all of your contact information is current, accurate, and professional.

Social networking sites often have a mechanism for you to connect with others, and in most cases, doing this requires the other person to accept your invitation. Be sure to initiate such an invitation with a courteous, respectful approach, recognizing that if the other person chooses to connect with you, it's comparable to the risk he or she faces when recommending you to others. This isn't a trivial decision, so be sure that your profile and your request are presented in a manner that gives the other person confidence that you will represent yourself—and him or her—well.

YOUR RESUME ESTABLISHES YOUR PERSONAL BRAND

As you progress through your degree, your resume and cover letter will serve as a tangible representation of your personal brand—who you are, what you know, what you can do, and how you're different from your peers and other individuals competing for the same jobs. Just as McDonald's, Apple, and the Gap invest significant effort and resources to define themselves through distinctive brands, so you need to establish a distinctive personal brand that makes you recognizable and relevant to organizations that need a talented workforce.

If you'd like to learn more about developing your personal brand, consult Tim O'Brien's (2007) book *The Power of Personal Branding*. It's a great resource for this important topic (www.thepersonalbrandinggroup.com).

Your Resume Puts Your Life on Paper

Learning to write a resume is an essential skill for a new college graduate, and there is no time like the present to begin honing that skill. Your resume is no place to be modest, but neither is it a place to embellish or misrepresent your skills or experience. All individuals have something—whether it's the classes they've taken, the projects they've completed, or the hardships they've overcome in their personal lives—that makes them special and

INTEGRITY *Matters*

While you may be excited to list your accomplishments on your resume, you must be sure not to go overboard in describing what you have done. A good rule to follow is to always provide accurate, truthful information in your resume and cover letter. Highlight your accomplishments without exaggerating them.

Lying on a resume is called "resume padding," and it can get you in serious trouble. At the very least, if a prospective employer discovers what you've done, you might not get the job. At the very worst, you might get fired after you are hired if the company finds out that your resume contains false information.

YOUR TURN

In approximately 250 words, describe where you think the line exists between making your accomplishments noteworthy and exaggerating them. Discuss what steps you will take to ensure that all the information on your resume and cover letter is accurate.

that gives them the experience and personal qualities that are important to an employer. The challenge is to describe those qualities in a resume and to do it in no more than a page, for most job applications.

A number of university-affiliated websites provide guidance on how to develop an effective resume. Your university's career services office will offer support resources, as well.

To get started, here's a basic list of what your resume should include:

- *Your name and contact information, including your address, phone number, and email address:* Make sure your voicemail has an appropriate message on it and that your email is professional, as well. An address like ejcantu@abcmail.com is preferable to one like bananafreak72@chunkymonkey.com.

- *A clear objective or purpose statement that describes your career goals:* The objective doesn't have to be written in a complete sentence. You may want to develop versions of your resume with different purpose statements so that you can personalize what you send to different companies in different industries.

- *Information about your educational accomplishments:* If you haven't yet completed your degree, write down the anticipated date: "Bachelor of Arts, May 2016." Also be sure to include any other certificates or degrees that you have earned.

- *Information about your work history:* List your most recent job first, and for each job, include the dates you worked, your position or title, the name and location of the company, and a bulleted list of your responsibilities. Describe your responsibilities using action verbs, such as *organized, developed, implemented,* and *managed.*

- *Extracurricular activities, organizations, or awards:* If you received a college scholarship, participated in a fundraising event, organized a community meeting, coached a sport, sat on a committee at your church or synagogue, or volunteered at your child's school, list these activities to demonstrate your accomplishments and contributions to society. Also be sure to list college-related accomplishments, such as making the dean's list and being a leader of or participating in student government and organizations.

- *A list of references:* As you meet and get to know people in college, consider adding their names to a list of potential references. For instance, a professor that you have gotten to know well, the advisor that you see each semester as you plan your degree, and a campus official that you have worked closely with on a project are all good candidates for writing letters of recommendation or serving as references. People you have worked with—either on the job or through a community project—are other excellent possibilities for references. Getting a person's permission before you list him or her on your resume is essential to getting a good reference.

- *A cover letter:* This letter accompanies your resume and explains in detail how your qualifications match what the employer is looking for. Like a resume, a cover letter should be brief and to the point—usually no more than a page. The more concise your resume and cover letter, the easier it will be for potential employers to determine whether you are right for the job.

As you consider what content to include in your resume, think of it as a body of evidence to support every claim you would want to make about yourself in an interview. If you believe that you are a hard-working person, then your resume should illustrate how you've managed to work during college. If you're an effective communicator, then your resume must be well written. It could also reference the high grades you've received in your composition and technical writing classes or that you participated in a high school debate team.

CASE SCENARIOS

1. Rudy is getting a degree in business management, but he doesn't have any idea how to look for a good job. In fact, he isn't really even sure if his degree is what he needs to break into financial planning, which is the career he believes will give him the financial stability that he values. Rudy has decided to use his connections with his classmates and professors to meet with a dozen different people at banks and financial institutions and to find out what it will take to get a job and succeed. It will take a few weeks to complete the interviews, but he knows that he will have time after he graduates and before he really gets serious about looking for a job.

    Use the following scale to rate the decision that has been made (1 = Poor Decision, 5 = Excellent Decision). Be prepared to explain your answer.

    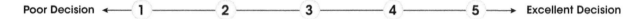
    Poor Decision ← 1 — 2 — 3 — 4 — 5 → Excellent Decision

2. Brian's dream is to own a horse farm, but he doesn't think he can afford his dream. That's why he's in his second semester as a radiology technician; it's a job with a steady income. Also, Brian doesn't want to quit school to follow his dream, because he values having an education. He realizes that as a radiology technician, he can make enough money to save up to purchase a horse farm on his own, but it will take at least 10 years of saving and planning before that will happen. Brian thinks he can endure the long hours and stressful work to make his dream come true eventually.

    Use the following scale to rate the decision that has been made (1 = Poor Decision, 5 = Excellent Decision). Be prepared to explain your answer.

    Poor Decision ← 1 — 2 — 3 — 4 — 5 → Excellent Decision

3. Lakeshia is ready to graduate with a degree in computer networking, and she has been circulating her resume with the hope that she will roll right into a job after graduation. Because Lakeshia lacks experience in this field, she has decided to elaborate on some of her responsibilities as a work study student in the information technology department and as an intern at a local advertising company. While she did provide assistance in both roles, she had few responsibilities and did not complete the kinds of projects she has listed on her resume. Lakeshia has decided to send out her resume with the exaggerations intact, because she is looking for out-of-state jobs and believes no one will find out that she's misrepresented her qualifications and experience.

    Use the following scale to rate the decision that has been made (1 = Poor Decision, 5 = Excellent Decision). Be prepared to explain your answer

    Poor Decision ← 1 — 2 — 3 — 4 — 5 → Excellent Decision

Take It with You

Action Item	Deadline	First Step
Identify potential careers that match your values, goals, and interests.		
Meet with a career counselor and some of your professors to discuss your career goals and employment strategy.		
Implement a networking strategy.		
Write your resume and review it with others.		
Practice interviewing for a job.		

REFERENCES

Bolles, R. (2011). *What color is your parachute? 2012: A practical manual for job-hunters and career-changers.* New York, NY: Ten Speed Press.

Darling, D. (2010). *The networking survival guide, second edition: Practical advice to help you gain confidence, approach people, and get the success you want,* New York, NY: McGraw Hill.

O'Brien, T. (2007). *The power of personal branding.* Los Angeles, CA: Mendham Publishing.

PHOTO CREDIT

Fotolia

Index